The Secret Identity of the Beloved Disciple

Joseph A. Grassi

PAULIST PRESS
New York/Mahw

D0181793

Library of Congress Cataloging-in-Publication Data

Grassi, Joseph A.
    The secret identity of the Beloved Disciple / by Joseph A. Grassi.
      p. cm.
    Includes bibliographical references.
    ISBN 0-8091-3121-8
    1. Beloved Disciple. 2. Bible. N.T. John—Biography. 3. Bible.
N.T. John—Criticism, interpretation, etc. I. Title.
    BS2452.B36G73 1990
    226.5'092—dc20   89-38000
                                                    CIP

Published by Paulist Press
997 Macarthur Boulevard
Mahwah, New Jersey 07430

Printed and bound in the United States of America

Contents

Contents

Introduction

Near the beginning of the second century, an exciting new document, now called John's gospel, began to circulate among Christian communities. It was strikingly different from other known gospels which placed heavy emphasis on church authority based on Peter and the twelve. In contrast, this new gospel gave priority to an inner authority based on Jesus' last gift, the Paraclete or Holy Spirit. This "fourth gospel" contained none of the ethical teachings of Jesus on money, marriage, divorce, etc. so prominent in the other gospels. Instead, all was reduced to one command of Jesus: to love one another.

While miracle stories abounded in other gospels, this document contained seven principal mysterious signs whose inner meaning was a deep understanding of Jesus and an intimate relationship with him. Where other gospels portrayed Jesus as a man and only hinted at his divinity, this one came to a climax with Thomas' confession, "My Lord and my God." Only in this gospel does Jesus openly proclaim himself as God with the words, "I and the Father are one." At times Jesus hardly appears to be a man at all, so overwhelming is the presentation of his divinity.

The authority behind this new gospel was an eyewitness "disciple whom Jesus loved," about whom previous sources had been mysteriously silent. This disciple was so close to Jesus that he reclined at the Lord's bosom at the last supper. He was the first one to know Jesus' greatest secret—that of his coming death through the betrayal of Judas. He was also the first to believe in Jesus' resurrection on seeing the empty tomb. While Peter is pre-

1

sented as an external successor to Jesus among the apostles, this disciple is portrayed as an inner successor, sharing the Lord's secrets and understanding the meaning of the master's death.

This gospel quickly became a favorite with early "offbeat" Christian communities who found in it support for their suspicion of external authority, and for their emphasis on inner experience. However, more conservative-minded Christians found this quite unsettling. Consequently, an unknown author composed a "balancing" document in the form of three letters of "John." These letters emphasized external works, warned against inner experience of the divinity, and stressed Jesus' humanity. In contrast to the gentle loving attitude of the gospels, the letters threatened severe punishments on non-conforming Christians, including excommunication.

With the "addition" of the letters, the gospel and the letters took on the appearance of a composite whole especially when they were circulated together. In this way, "radical" verses of the gospel could be understood and interpreted through much more conservative statements in the letters. As a result, church authorities now felt that the total work could be safely used even to counteract those "far out" Christians who had so welcomed the gospel itself.

However, the authorship was a problem. Church leaders based their own authority on succession to the twelve. Who was this "beloved disciple" who claimed so much authority in this document? By the end of the second century, important bishops identified him as John, brother of James, a son of Zebedee and one of the twelve apostles. This brought the author (who was considered the beloved disciple) into the top ring of the church's external authority. It also provided an additional way to modify and harmonize the gospel's more radical statements on inner experience and authority. This identification of the author with one of the apostles also made it possible for the previously "suspicious" work to be made part of the official approved canon of the church's inspired writings.

However, even in the early church, doubts were raised about this identification of the beloved disciple with John, son of Zebedee. Yet practically all Christians, guided by church authority, eventually accepted it until the nineteenth century and the beginnings of modern scientific study of the Bible. Since that time, more and more difficulties have been raised against this identification.

Despite the scholarly investigations of almost two centuries, the identity of the beloved disciple has remained one of the greatest mysteries in the Bible. However, the detective-like work of scripture scholars has been slowly accumulating a file of valuable clues, although some of them are admittedly very slight and even ridiculous at first glance. Yet Paul Minear[1] in his own study of the beloved disciple has aptly remarked:

> Over the centuries the search for the beloved disciple has been so intense and so wide-ranging that it is an act of consummate audacity to suggest a new thesis for consideration. Yet no one is wholly content with the present solutions of the riddle, and the issue is of such central importance that it would be wrong to call off the search entirely. That search requires the careful reexamination of every clue, however fanciful at first sight.

My intention is first to assemble and evaluate the clues so far advanced; secondly, it is to add new clues drawn from hidden literary codes both in John's gospel and in its background in the Hebrew scriptures. The end result, I submit, will be an exciting new perspective on the beloved disciple—first, as a person with an unusual relationship to Jesus and inner understanding of him; second, as one of the greatest creative and mystical geniuses in the history of Christianity.

1
The Illusion of John the Apostle, Son of Zebedee as the Beloved Disciple

It is no light matter to lay aside a cherished tradition of the Christian church for almost two thousand years. The source of this tradition is twofold: external authorities of the first two centuries and internal evidence from the gospel itself. As regards external authorities, we note that the gospel of John first saw light around 100 C.E.[2] Hints of its influence are found in the letters of Ignatius[3] around 110 C.E. and in Justin,[4] but no solid quotation of it is found until Theophilus of Antioch[5] (about 180 C.E.) who quotes John 1:1 as scripture. By the end of the second century and the beginning of the third, most church writers identified the evangelist and beloved disciple (taken together) as John the apostle. However, there were some doubts raised: Papias,[6] bishop of Hierapolis (about 150 C.E.), seems to distinguish between two Johns from whom he had heard—John the apostle and John the presbyter.

In regard to these early testimonies, it must be kept in mind that sharp divisions began to appear within the Christian church toward the beginning of the second century C.E. A witness to this is the huge work *Against the Heresies* written by Irenaeus, bishop of Lyon, around 180 C.E. For writers like Irenaeus, it was essential to establish their authority as successors of the twelve apostles of Jesus and thus qualified to decide what was authentic Christian doctrine.

When the fourth gospel began to circulate, it appealed

strongly to "unorthodox" groups of Christians. The latter were impressed by its emphasis on the priority of the authority of the Holy Spirit and inner experience in contrast to external church authority. The first commentary on the gospel was made by a gnostic-oriented writer called Heracleon[7] around 170 C.E. Because such groups found so much support in this gospel, another writer[8] found it necessary to compose several "letters of John" to counteract some of the radical interpretations some people were making of that gospel. Gradually, the gospel and letters came to be regarded as a unified whole from one author. In this way, the more radical statements of the gospel could be interpreted and harmonized by those in the letters. As a result, the composite work could now be used by orthodox church leaders to counter the very groups among whom the gospel was so popular.

A final step in establishing the orthodoxy of the fourth gospel was its attribution to John, one of the twelve. This placed it squarely among the authority structures of the church: an apostle had composed it; therefore the bishops and successors of the apostles could interpret its meaning. This, of course, leads us to some suspicion about the motives of early orthodox church writers in their common attribution of the gospel to John the apostle. R.E. Brown, a leading Johannine scholar, first defended the authorship of John the apostle in his Anchor Bible Commentary.[9] However, he changed his views in his *The Community of the Beloved Disciple* some thirteen years later, and made this comment:

> By setting the Beloved Disciple over against Peter . . . the Fourth Gospel gives the impression that he was an outsider to the group of best-known disciples, a group that would have included John son of Zebedee. . . . The external (late second-century) evidence identifying the Beloved Disciple as John is a further step in a direction, already visible in the NT itself, toward simplifying Christian origins by reduction to the Twelve Apostles.[10]

However, John the apostle's place as author and beloved disciple rested not only on external authority but on internal "proofs" within the gospels: John and James, sons of Zebedee and apostles, are not mentioned by name in the fourth gospel. However, in the other three gospels, Peter, John and James are the "big three," sometimes joined by Andrew, the brother of Peter. They were the closest persons to Jesus and privileged with his special secrets—e.g. his transfiguration (Mk 9:2), his agony in the garden (Mk 14:33) and his prophecy of the temple destruction (Mk 13:3). John is mentioned more often than any other apostle except Peter. Therefore the most logical candidate for the beloved disciple among people known by name in the four gospels would be John, son of Zebedee and one of the twelve apostles.

As a result of these external and internal arguments, John the apostle was commonly accepted as both the beloved disciple and author of the fourth gospel until the nineteenth century and the beginnings of modern scientific Bible study. Even today it still is the popular view of most Christians. However, important clues in other directions continued to appear in scholarly circles. Pierson Parker[11] in the early 1960s criticized the continued support of the ancient view and enumerated many features of the beloved disciple that did not match John the apostle. The following are some arguments brought out by Parker and other critics:

1. John the son of Zebedee was a Galilean, yet the beloved disciple appears to be a Judaean, making his first explicit gospel entry at Jesus' last supper (Jn 13:23). Jesus called John by the Lake of Galilee where the apostle was a fisherman (Mk 1:16–20). The beloved disciple, however, is well known in Jerusalem, at least in the high priest's household (Jn 18:15–17). The fourth gospel has unusual details about Jerusalem and its environs but few about Galilee, which would certainly be the region John the apostle knew best.
2. In Mark, Jesus called James and John "sons of thunder" (Mk 3:17). They appear to be bold men of action. In Luke, the two brothers wish to call down lightning on Samaritans who did not receive Jesus. Jesus in turn rebukes them for their improper attitude (9:51–56). This portrayal does not fit the mild

image of the beloved disciple in the fourth gospel which is especially sympathetic to Samaritans (4:1–42).

3. In the fourth gospel there is no mention of any kind of exorcism or interest in it. In the other gospels, Jesus as well as the apostles (Mk 6:13) frequently cast out demons. John the apostle seems especially concerned about this power. On one occasion he was concerned that someone outside the twelve was casting out demons in Jesus' name, and even forbade him to do so (Mk 9:38–41).

4. In regard to Peter and John the apostle, it is always Peter who takes the initiative and is the spokesman (Acts 1:13–15; 3:1–7; 8:14–24). However, in the fourth gospel it is the beloved disciple who takes the initiative, not Peter. The beloved disciple is called before Peter (1:35–41); Peter has to ask him to request information about the traitor from Jesus (13:23–26). The beloved disciple precedes Peter to the tomb and believes before he does (20:4, 5, 8).

5. The beloved disciple was familiar with the house and family of the high priest Annas in Jerusalem, even gaining admittance for Peter by speaking with the maid (18:15–17). This is hard to imagine of John the apostle, a fisherman from Galilee. This John was also brought before the same high priest in Acts 4:5–23. The high priest does not seem to know him and treats him as if he were a stranger.

6. John the apostle was present at events that would have been very important for the fourth gospel, yet there is no mention of them: for example the transfiguration (Mk 9:2) and the raising of the daughter of Jairus (Mk 5:37).

In conclusion, the images of John the apostle and the beloved disciple that are presented in the gospels are so strikingly different that Parker makes the following conclusion:

> The NT presents many facets of this John's character, and of his experience. *Not one of them is reflected in the Fourth Gospel.* For John the son of Zebedee to have written this book,

the personality which he brought before Jesus would have had
to be not transformed, but blotted out.[12]

While much scholarly work has been done since the time of
Parker, and some modification of his conclusion may be necessary, his basic premises have not been seriously challenged.

Was the Gospel Author the Same as the Beloved Disciple?

We have noted that ancient tradition did not distinguish the
beloved disciple and the gospel author. They were both John the
apostle. Is this necessarily so? There is no question of physical
impossibility. The beloved disciple may have been very young
during Jesus' ministry and lived on until a ripe old age. There is no
doubt that many scenes in the fourth gospel have the distinct signs
of the reminiscences of an eyewitness, who would be the beloved
disciple. For example, when a soldier pierced Jesus' side at the
cross, the author writes, "He who saw it bears witness and he
knows his witness is true" (19:35).

However, there are distinct signs in some gospel pericopes
that the author is not an eyewitness, but is drawing upon previous
written or oral sources. For example, modern scholarship[13] has
brought forth strong reasons to believe that the story of Jesus'
anointing at Bethany in John 12:1–8 is drawn from several other
accounts: that of an anointing of Jesus' *feet* by a penitent woman
(Lk 7:36–50) and a last anointing of Jesus' head at the house of
Simon the leper (Mk 14:1–9). Into these two stories the author
has inserted Martha, Mary and Lazarus as a link with the resurrection of Lazarus in chapter 11. Such complex literary work could
hardly be that of the blessed disciple as an eyewitness and close
associate of Jesus.

Another indicator that the beloved disciple is not the author
is found in chapter 21, a possible appendix to the gospel. In this
chapter it is presumed that Peter has already died, and it is related
that his martyr death was predicted by Jesus (21:18–19). As if in
parallel to this, Peter asks Jesus about the beloved disciple who is

following them also. Jesus said to Peter, "If it is my will that he remain until I come, what is that to you? Follow me!" (20:22). The writer then notes the following, "The saying spread abroad among the brethren that this disciple was not to die; yet Jesus did not say to him that he was not to die, but, 'If it is my will that he remain until I come, what is that to you?' " Given the parallel to the death of Peter, the meaning seems to be that the beloved disciple has died, and that this has created a difficulty for the gospel audience in view of their recollection of this saying of Jesus. However, the writer wishes to correct this misunderstanding and emphasize that Jesus' statement was conditional: *If* it is my will that he remain until I come" (21:22). In chapter 14 we shall make additional observations about the relationship of chapter 21 to the rest of the gospel.

Consequently, I will assume in this work that the final author and beloved disciple are two different people. Yet, it is evident that the author is a close disciple of the beloved disciple and faithfully mirrors his master and teacher. This is done in so close a manner that it is extremely difficult to separate in the gospel what belongs to the beloved disciple and what results from the evangelist. In any case, the beloved disciple is the *authority* behind the fourth gospel that was all-important for the gospel audience. Modern literary criticism[14] has presented a strong case that the gospel as it now stands forms a very careful literary unity which made sense both to the author and to his audience. It is from this viewpoint that we will study this gospel.

2
Qualifications of Other Candidates for an Unusual Position

While some of these candidates may be admittedly "dark horses," their evaluation will be helpful in our search by way of comparison.

Lazarus—"The one whom you love is sick" (11:3)

This designation of Lazarus is like that of the beloved disciple who is five times called the disciple, or the one whom Jesus loved (13:23; 19:26; 20:2; 21:7, 20). The verb used in 11:3 is *philō* corresponding to 20:2. The other texts use *agapaō* of the beloved disciple. The different verbs may not be significant because *agapaō* is also used of Lazarus in 11:5 where it is related that Jesus loved Martha and her sister and Lazarus. The special love of Jesus for Lazarus is also described in 11:36 where the Jews say, "See how much he [Jesus] loved him." J.N. Sanders[15] has pointed out a number of clues that might identify Lazarus with the beloved disciple: Lazarus is from Bethany near Jerusalem (11:1), corresponding to the beloved disciple's familiarity with and closeness to the capital city.

The raising of Lazarus is a supreme act of devotion, for Jesus risked his life to go into Judea in order to raise him up (11:7–11). At Bethany, Lazarus was at a banquet with Jesus six days before the Passover (12:1) just as the beloved disciple was with Jesus at the supper (13:23). The saying of Jesus, "If it is my will that he

11

remain until I come, what is that to you?" (21:22) would be under-
standable if referring to Lazarus whom Jesus had already raised
from the dead, and therefore, perhaps preserved from a second
death. It would also be fitting that someone raised from the dead
would be the first to believe in Jesus' resurrection (20:8) and
recognize him in a post-resurrection apparition.

Sanders' suggestion is not unique to him alone but follows
that of Filson[16] and others.

In response, there are a number of decided weaknesses in
these arguments that should be pointed out: Jesus' love for Lazarus does not seem to be singled out but is part of his love for that
family: he loves Martha and Mary his sisters as well (11:5); he
comes to Judea at their request, and raises up Lazarus after Martha and Mary speak to him. The presence of Lazarus as well as
Mary and Martha at the Bethany banquet, as pointed out in the
last chapter, is probably a conflation from various sources. Since
this explicit mention of Lazarus was never connected with the
beloved disciple by any writers of the first centuries, it is a sign
that it was not so perceived by the audience of this gospel, who
probably did not need to be told who the beloved disciple was.
Finally, except at the foot of the cross (since Peter had fled), every
time the beloved disciple is named in chapters 13, 18, 20 and 21,
Peter is also mentioned by way of comparison or contrast. However, in chapters 11 and 12, in all the places Lazarus is mentioned,
Peter is not named. This would not fit the beloved disciple in his
close association with Peter.

"John, whose name was Mark" (Acts 12:12)

Luke, in his Acts of the Apostles, tells us that the early
Jerusalem church had an important meeting place in Jerusalem at
the "house of Mary, the mother of John, who was called Mark"
(Acts 12:12). Paul and Barnabas took him with them from Jerusalem (12:25) and brought him along on their first missionary journey. However, "John left them and returned to Jerusalem"
(13:13) when they were in Pamphylia. On a second journey, Bar-

nabas wished to take along John, but Paul refused; this resulted in such a bitter argument that Barnabas left Paul and took "Mark" with him to Cyprus (15:39). Colossians 4:10 notes that John-Mark was also a cousin of Barnabas.

At first glance, John-Mark has much more in his favor than Lazarus. In suggesting that the beloved disciple was this young man, Pierson Parker[17] notes that he came from a prominent Christian family in Jerusalem that was known in the early years of the church. As a relative of Barnabas, who was a Levite (Acts 4:36), he would probably be from a priestly family himself, thus fitting the description of the beloved disciple as someone known to the high priest's household (Jn 18:15). Also, there is an unusual description only in Mark of a young disciple who kept following Jesus after all the apostles left him and fled. He was seized but fled away naked (Mk 14:15). This would fit the beloved disciple who followed Jesus although all the others fled. More will be noted on this mysterious verse in chapter 12.

Once more, there are serious difficulties with this identification. In the first centuries this John-Mark was connected with the gospel of Mark, and never with that of John. We might add that the two gospels are so strikingly different that it is impossible to think of the same author behind both of them. Also, this John-Mark seems to be quite a minor figure in the Acts of the Apostles as compared to both Paul and Barnabas. We saw that Paul did not even wish to take him along on his second journey. This secondary place would hardly fit a person who held such a close connection to Jesus as the beloved disciple and whose testimony about the death of Jesus was so important to the community addressed by the gospel.

John the Presbyter

We know of this John the presbyter from the fragments of Papias, a bishop of Hierapolis in Asia Minor, who wrote around 130 C.E. The fragments are found in the writings of Irenaeus and Eusebius, the church historian.[18] Papias has the following:

Whenever anyone came my way who had been a follower of the elders *(presbyteroi)*, I asked about the sayings of the elders: What did Andrew or Peter say? Or Philip or Thomas, or James, or John or Matthew or any other of the Lord's disciples and what did Aristion or John the elder (presbyter), disciples of the Lord, say.[19]

In this quotation we note the distinction between John the apostle and another John the presbyter from whom Papias had heard. This was a distinction elaborated on by Eusebius in whom the fragment is found. Irenaeus calls him a disciple of John.[20]

By way of response, this John the presbyter remains a shadowy figure. No early church writings claim that he is the author of the gospel of John, although Jerome states that he may be the author of the second and third letters of John.[21] Although Irenaeus and others speak of Papias as a disciple of this John, it would be next to impossible that Papias knew him while still alive in 130 C.E. It seems that Papias is speaking of followers of John the presbyter from whom he had heard, not John himself. This John the presbyter is credited with unusual teachings about the millennium: that each grape, e.g., would yield twenty-five measures of wine![22] Such teachings are not in accord with John's gospel. Along with the lack of any early testimonies they make John the presbyter a rather weak candidate for the beloved disciple. Finally, it should be mentioned that Papias nowhere makes the claim that this John the presbyter was the author of the fourth gospel.

The Beloved Disciple as a Representative Figure

In this hypothesis, the beloved disciple is not a real person at all but a representative figure. Many proposals have been made about whom he represents. Some of the principal ones are the following: that the beloved disciple represents the prophetic role of the Johannine school that wrote the gospel.[23] Another is that of Bultmann[24] who suggested that the beloved disciple represents the Greek Christian church. In this case, Jesus leaves his mother (Jewish Christianity) in the care of his beloved disciple (19:26) who represents this Hellenistic church. Schweizer considered the beloved disciple as a sign of the faith bond between every believer and the Lord.[25] Also, it has been proposed that the beloved disciple represents Gentile Christianity in opposition to Peter standing for Jewish Christianity.

None of the above proposals have presented strong enough reasons to warrant a detailed study. However, more serious is the suggestion that the beloved disciple represents the ideal Christian believer. This proposal has been frequently made, beginning with Loisy.[26] This identification demands special consideration since there are definite signs in the gospel that this symbolic element is present.

The following are indications that the beloved disciple does represent the ideal believer. He is most frequently "the one, or the disciple whom Jesus loved" (13:23; 19:26; 20:2; 21:7, 20). This is indeed a description of Jesus' relationship to any Christian. For example, Jesus loves Lazarus, Martha, and Mary (11:5). When Lazarus is seriously ill, his sisters send word to Jesus, "He whom you love is sick" (11:3). The story itself stands for Jesus' action in regard to raising up from the dead all believers whom he loves in the same way. In addition, "beloved" is a frequent address to Christians found in many of the New Testament letters, including those of Paul, John, and Peter.

The description of the disciple at the bosom of Jesus (13:23, 25; 21:20) also may have a symbolic sense. Jesus abides at the bosom of the Father: "The only Son, who is in the bosom of the Father, he has made him known" (1:18). Thus he is able to reveal his Father's love to all believers who likewise come to Jesus in an intimate relationship (at his bosom) and learn from him. The beloved disciple followed Jesus to the cross and never denied him—a symbol of the believer willing to risk his life for the master. The beloved disciple came to the empty tomb (20:8) and believed (without the help of apparitions) that Jesus had indeed risen. This is what every believer must do: the empty tomb is enough. The beloved disciple recognizes Jesus in the miraculous draught of fish (21:7). This seems to represent the conversions that come about in the church through Jesus' word. Like the beloved disciple, the believer will see in this a sign of Jesus' presence.

A symbolic meaning for the beloved disciple is strengthened by the author's penchant for bringing out representative meanings for various other characters in the gospel. Thomas in 20:24–29 is a "doubting Thomas" for all time, standing for those who will not believe unless they have physical, tangible proofs: "Unless I see in his hands the print of the nails, and place my finger in the mark of the nails, and place my hand in his side, I will not believe" (20:25). The author himself seals the representative meaning with the conclusion, "Blessed are those who have not seen and yet believe" (20:29). Judas at the last supper (13:2, 27, 30) represents those Christians who are present at worship, but do not really believe in their hearts. Like Judas, Satan enters their hearts (13:2) and they go out in darkness (13:30). Lazarus stands for any Christian believer who can be brought to life through the resurrection of Jesus. Jesus is the resurrection and the life (11:25) in face of the terrible power of death. The question addressed to Martha, "Do you believe this?" (11:26), is really addressed to the gospel audience. The man cured of blindness from birth seems to be an "everyman," for Jesus says in conclusion, "For judgment I have come into this world, that those who do not see may see, and that those who see may become blind" (9:39).

Another approach to the beloved disciple is based on the discovery of the dramatic literary quality of the fourth gospel. In this literary view, using the words of Alan Culpepper,

> The narrative world of the gospel is neither a window on the ministry of Jesus nor a window on the history of the Johannine community. Primarily, at least, it is the literary creation of the evangelist, which is crafted with the purpose of leading readers to "see" the world as the evangelist sees it.[27]

This literary approach, especially the work of Culpepper, has yielded many valuable insights on the meaning of the gospel of John. However, it profoundly affects the historical nature of the gospel characters. In regard to the beloved disciple, it means that he is an "idealized characterization of an historical figure . . . because of his significance for the community, the Beloved Disciple was idealized by the author and given a role at the last supper, the crucifixion, the discovery of the empty tomb, and the appearance in Galilee."[28]

In response, it must be said that if the beloved disciple is only an ideal figure or an "idealized characterization of an historical figure" the whole credibility of this document is in jeopardy. The author is appealing to an eyewitness of important events who relates them so that others might believe also. One such event was the moment of Jesus' death and the unusual flow of watery blood that came from his side. The author gives very special importance to this with the words, "He who saw it has borne witness—his testimony is true, and he knows that he tells the truth—that you also may believe" (19:35). If the beloved disciple, who is described as being present when this happened (19:25), is merely a symbolic or representative figure, this destroys the trustworthiness of the gospel by presenting an imaginary witness. It also attacks the credibility of Christianity itself which has taken this gospel and placed it in its official canon of inspired books that deal with the origins of faith. So R.E. Brown[29] writes,

> The thesis that he is purely fictional or only an ideal figure is quite implausible. It would mean that the author of John 21:20–23 was deceived or deceptive, for he reports distress in the community over the Beloved Disciple's death. The Disciple was idealized, of course; but in my judgment the fact that he was a historical person and a companion of Jesus becomes all the more obvious in the new approaches to Johannine ecclesiology. Later in community history when the Johannine Christians were clearly distinct from groups of Christians who associated themselves with memories of the Twelve (e.g., with the memory of Peter), the claim to possess the witness of the Beloved Disciple enabled the Johannine Christians to defend their peculiar insights in christology and ecclesiology.

This does not mean that the beloved disciple cannot be *both* an historical figure as well as a symbol of the ideal believer. The author intends his audience to identify with the figures in his gospel. Judas, for example, can be an actual person whose betrayal of Jesus set into action the course of events that would lead to Jesus' saving death (13:30–31). At the same time, each reader is a "Judas" when taking part in the Lord's supper without proper belief. So there is no question of "either a symbolic or an actual figure." The beloved disciple is an actual historical witness that guarantees the Johannine community the truths they believe in. At the same time, the gospel writer presents him as a symbolic figure with which every person in his audience can identify.

By way of summary: In this chapter we have examined the credentials of other candidates for the beloved disciple. The most important of these are Lazarus, John the presbyter, John-Mark, and the representative believer. Lazarus and John-Mark simply do not have enough clues to make an identification, and in addition decidedly differ from the gospel portrait. John the presbyter is intriguing as coming from an ancient source pointing to another John not the son of Zebedee. However, he remains a nebulous figure with little known about him. As regards a purely representative figure, the whole credibility of the gospel and New Testament would be thrown into jeopardy if the gospel references to the beloved disciple as an eyewitness are a hoax. However, there are strong indications that the beloved disciple is a representative figure *as well as* an historical person.

The trail of clues in this chapter has led to important results, though by way of elimination: *None of these "suspects" have enough credentials to claim the place of the beloved disciple. However, his partial role as a representative figure has a high degree of probability.* At this point, it looks as if an impasse has been reached. However, when such a point occurs, a good detective does not abandon the search but looks in entirely new directions where there are often many surprises in store. This process will begin in our next two chapters where new perspectives on the background and role of the beloved disciple will lead us to valuable new clues.

3
The Role and Community
of the Beloved Disciple

The only reliable way to know this mysterious figure is through the actual document behind which he is the dominant figure. What are the characteristics and beliefs of the gospel audience? What is the author trying to get across to them? Do his beliefs coincide with theirs? What differences if any are there? Other questions to be raised are the following: What is the relationship of the beloved disciple to that audience? What kind of credibility does he have for the things that he writes to them? What relationship does he have with Jesus? In trying to establish the identity of the beloved disciple, modern scholars have given special attention to the actual role that he plays in regard to his audience instead of first trying to find out who he really is.

Raymond E. Brown is prominent among the leading scholars[30] who have given special attention to the beloved disciple's role vis-à-vis the various groups addressed by the gospel. In addition to his three monumental Anchor Bible volumes on the gospel and the letters of John, his book *The Community of the Beloved Disciple* focuses on this question, giving his own views as well as summarizing the work of other scholars. Much of what we have to say in this chapter owes its inspiration to his work, although not limited to it or always in accord with it.

By way of background, some seventy years or so had passed between Jesus' death and the publication of the gospel. Third generation Christians were now living. During this time period there was much development in Christian reflection especially in regard to the person of Christ. Some Christian teachers moved toward a "high" christology, meaning such an exalted view of Jesus' person that he could be called "God." This is the view of the gospel writer and the "school" or community with which he is intimately associated. We might call this "the Johannine community." We find this exalted view in the gospel prologue which soars like an eagle into the lofty heights of meditation and proclaims Jesus as the eternal word of God (1:1). It is also found in the climactic moment of the gospel when Thomas confesses that Jesus is God with the words, "My Lord and my God" (20:28).

In addition, some Christians went even further in their beliefs and speculations. Their ideas about Christ became so exalted that his humanity suffered in consequence. In this way, doubts arose about the reality of his sufferings and even his death. Christ appeared to them as hardly one of us, except for appearances. This type of thinking is called docetism, and is one of the characteristics of gnostic views of Jesus. The gospel of John, with its high christology, its triumphant view of the risen Christ and its inner emphasis, was a favorite with such groups. We saw in an earlier chapter that the first commentary on John was written by a gnostic called Heracleon.

To counter such groups and bring them into harmony, our author places strong emphasis on the reality of the sacrificial death of Jesus, witnessing his actual death along with the additional lethal spear thrust (19:30–34). Jesus' human feelings are noted: his tiredness at the Samaria well (4:6); his sadness and weeping at the death of Lazarus (11:33–35). However, it seems that this was not enough to counteract gnostic and docetic tendencies. The letters of "John" were added as an antidote to such teachings with strong statements such as, "Every spirit which confesses that Jesus Christ has come in the flesh is of God, and every spirit which does not confess Jesus is not of God" (1 Jn 4:2).

On the other side of the spectrum, there were Christians whose thinking and beliefs about Christ had not progressed through the years. They still clung to a very limited christology, seeing in Jesus little more than the promised messiah of the Jews.

Among them were many former disciples of John the Baptist. After his death, his followers were found scattered about the Mediterranean world, where Christian preachers often came in contact with them and even controversy. For example, the Acts of the Apostles tells us that a certain Jew named Apollos came to Ephesus from Alexandria. He knew about Jesus, but only as connected with the baptism of John. Paul's colleagues, Priscilla and Aquila, gave him further instruction so that he could become a "full Christian" (18:24–26). When Paul came to Ephesus he found a group of former disciples of the Baptist who did not even know about the Holy Spirit and baptism. He instructed them and baptized them (19:1–6). It is quite evident that these "Baptists" did not know and believe in the saving effects of Jesus' death.

The beloved disciple was greatly concerned about these disciples of the Baptist (once again we state that the beloved disciple and the author are not the same, yet the author is so much his disciple that their thinking is hard to distinguish, except at the points we have indicated and others to come). The gospel has a strong link between the beloved disciple and the Baptist. The beloved disciple was a disciple of his before he came to know Jesus. The Baptist introduced him to Jesus, whose disciple he then became. (In a later chapter we will point out in detail how we can know this is the beloved disciple's call.) Thus we see that this disciple is someone very close to the Baptist as well as to Jesus— someone who can establish an important bond between the two for the gospel audience. The Baptist introduces Jesus with the words, "Behold, the Lamb of God," and earlier, "Behold the Lamb of God who takes away the sins of the world" (1:36; 1:29).

Later we will see in chapter 7 that the beloved disciple by the cross finally establishes that Jesus is the new passover lamb, thus completing and affirming the full meaning of the Baptist's words. Consequently, we can carefully note an important clue for further investigation: *The identity and role of the beloved disciple is closely linked to John the Baptist and his disciples.* In order to convince the Baptist's disciples in his audience, the author establishes the beloved disciple as a disciple and successor of the Baptist who completes and brings to full meaning his message. At the same time, the author carefully notes that John the Baptist was not the messiah (Christ) nor the expected returned Elijah the prophet (1:19–21). He is not the light who is to come into the world (1:6), not the bridegroom of the last times, but only his friend, who stands by and rejoices that he must decrease while the bridegroom increases (3:28–30).

A second group with limited beliefs in Jesus would be those Jewish Christians whose beliefs had not progressed through the years. They appealed to the authority of James, the brother of the Lord, for their credentials. James kept to the ancient rules for table fellowship that had separated the Jews and Gentiles for centuries. We see an example of this in Paul's letter to the Galatians where a group of Christians "from James" came to Antioch from Jerusalem and refused to eat together with Gentile Christians (2:11–12). These Christians indeed believed that Jesus was the messiah, but their views about his divinity were very limited. They based their belief on Jesus' miracles and signs. They thought of Jesus as a powerful wonder-worker like Moses. In memory of Jesus, they broke bread but tended to consider it a kind of "wonder-bread" like that of Moses in the desert of Sinai (Ex 16).

To address these Jewish Christians, the author does not emphasize Jesus' healings and miracles as such. Instead, they are only signs for disciples to reach a deep relationship with Jesus along with an appreciation of his saving death, as well as a belief in his divinity. The author (and the beloved disciple, his source) bring the passion account to a close and perhaps the gospel itself (if chapter 21 is an appendix) by stating the goal of Jesus' signs:

> Now Jesus did many other signs in the presence of the disciples which are not written in this book; but these are written that you may believe that Jesus is the Christ, the Son of God, and that believing you may have life in his name (20:30–31).

This emphasis on signs leads us to note another clue about him (the beloved disciple to whom the author owes his inspiration): *He is a mystic and creative genius who is able to look deeply into externals and find a deep meaning in the miracles of Jesus as well as in the "ordinary" events of his life. He will see in them the fruition of a secret divine plan found especially in the scriptures.* This aspect will be further developed in chapter 10. Along with perceiving the inner meaning of Jesus' miracles, the author will also show how the great Jewish feasts, Passover, Booths, and Pentecost, find their ultimate meaning in Jesus' saving death and its effects.

For the author and the beloved disciple, a central question would be the differences over the meaning of the breaking of bread. We will see in chapter 7 that this assumes a central place in the gospel. Many disciples part from Jesus after his difficult saying about the necessity of eating his flesh and drinking his blood (6:51–66). *This connection of the beloved disciple with the matter of Jesus' sign of the loaves in chapter 6 will also be an important clue we will follow in ascertaining the role and function of Jesus' favorite disciple.*

The above Jewish Christians openly professed their faith in Jesus as Messiah, despite their differences. However, there were others who still remained in the synagogue and concealed their faith in Jesus while still living to all appearances as Jews. They are perhaps represented in the gospel by Nicodemus, a Jewish teacher and member of the Sanhedrin who came to Jesus at night (3:2), and Joseph of Arimathea "who was a disciple of Jesus, but secretly, for fear of the Jews" (19:38). We note the motivation of fear or human respect that the evangelist mentions at this point. The author is trying to encourage them to come out into the open and profess their faith publicly. He describes Nicodemus and Joseph as claiming from Pilate Jesus' body at the risk of their lives in order to present an example of a conversion of what R. E. Brown calls "Crypto-Christians."[31]

At a middle point among the various Christians previously mentioned we find "apostolic Christians." These would be communities of mixed Gentiles and Jewish believers who looked to Peter and other members of the twelve as founders. They tended to be more highly organized, with their leaders considering themselves as authoritative successors to the twelve. They would be very much like those Christians addressed by Matthew's gospel where Peter's authority and that of the external church are greatly emphasized (cf. the passages on Peter's confession and church membership in 16:17–20; 18:18–20). These "apostolic Christians" believed in Jesus as Messiah, Son of God due to his Davidic descent and mysterious birth at Bethlehem as in Matthew 1:18–25. However they did not have the same lofty christology as the beloved disciple and the author of the fourth gospel with their disciples. In addition, they did not seem to have the same deep appreciation of the preeminence of the inner work of the Paraclete or Holy Spirit as in John's gospel. Their emphasis was more on the external witness of the church under the leadership of authoritative teachers.

Consequently, the fourth gospel strives to elevate these Christians to a higher christology by presenting Jesus as the eternal Word of God right from the opening words until the final explicit confession of Thomas in 20:28. To counterbalance the orientation of Petrine Christians to external authority the gospel devotes several chapters to the inner authority of the Holy Spirit or Paraclete (chapters 14–16). In practically all places where the beloved disciple is named Peter is also found, and his lack of inner understanding is contrasted with that of the beloved disciple. These texts will be taken up later in detail, but at present we can just note another clue: *the association of the beloved disciple with Peter and the contrasts between the two may point to the beloved disciple as an inner successor of Jesus while Peter is an "outer" successor.*

The following "line up" of various Christians addressed by the gospel may help summarize what we have just described:

1.	Baptist's Disciples	Very low christology, lack of understanding about Jesus' death.
2.A.	Jewish Christians	Low christology based on Jesus' signs; eucharist seen as "wonder-bread."

2.B.	Crypto-Christians	Jewish Christians remaining in synagogue because of fear.
3.	Apostolic Christians	Emphasis on external church teachers and succession of the twelve. "Medium christology" based on Jesus' extraordinary birth and Davidic descent.
4.	Johannine Community	Deep appreciation of Jesus' divinity and sacrificial implications of his death as applied to Jesus' difficult sayings about eating his flesh and blood.
5.	Extremists	Jesus' divinity at expense of his humanity. Overemphasis on "inner" experience. This group would have similarities to early Christian gnostics.

If we look at the above chart, the third group, apostolic Christians, represents a middle point. Groups 1 and 2 would be to the "right" as conserving as much as possible from Judaism or John the Baptist. Groups 4 and 5 would be to the "left" or more radical in emphasizing the differences between Judaism and Christianity through a deeper appreciation of Jesus' divinity as well as his death and resurrection. The gospel of John thus "leans to the left." We can well understand why it would be favored by "offbeat" Christians, and why it was necessary to balance it with the much more conservative "letters of John" where inner experience is downplayed and Jesus' humanity is given special emphasis.

In regard to the above groups what is the goal of the author (who depends on the authority of the beloved disciple)? Obviously he would like all groups to embrace the same outlook that he and his followers have in regard to Christ. However, his approach is not condemnatory. He openly states what he believes and contrasts it to what others hold. Yet he does so in a gentle way, appealing for oneness and communion. This theme of oneness occupies a central place in the gospel. In Jesus' final prayer he prays that "they may all be one; even as you, Father, are in me, and I in you, that they also may be in us, so that the world may believe that you have sent me" (17:21 and repeated in 17:23).

The author has Jesus as good shepherd recognize that there are such differences: "I have other sheep that are not of this fold; I must bring them also, and they will heed my voice. So there shall be one flock, one shepherd" (10:16). The purpose of Jesus' death is to "gather into one the children of God who are scattered abroad" (11:52). While we are not certain which groups these texts have in mind, they do show that oneness and communion are very much on the author's mind. Other hints of this oneness may also be present in the observation that there is no tear or "schism" in Jesus' garment before he is crucified (19:23). Also in the miraculous draught of fish, representing the fruits of missionary preaching, "although there were so many, the net was not torn" (21:11). In both of these texts the same Greek verb *schizō* is found.

Yet the basic question remains: How does the author hope to convince such widely divergent groups? Here is where we learn a great deal about the beloved disciple. The author must appeal to the witness of someone who was so close to Jesus that he can speak with an authoritative voice. So in his gospel he emphasizes five times that his source is the especially beloved disciple (13:23; 19:26; 20:2; 21:7, 20). At the last supper he has the most privileged spot at the bosom of Jesus (13:23). However, much more important is the actual relationship to Jesus. Other groups appealed to founders with very special connections with Jesus. Apostolic Christians could point to Peter the rock for support of their views. Jewish Christians prided themselves on the guidance of James, the brother of the Lord. What could be better than an actual family member or blood relative of Jesus who became the first leader of the Jerusalem community (Acts 15:13; 21:7; Gal

1:19; 2:9, 12)? Disciples of the Baptist appealed to the authority of someone who came even before Jesus and actually baptized him.

Consequently, the author must present his teacher with the strongest possible credentials—as someone so closely related to Jesus that he can be regarded as an authoritative successor to the master in a manner that would compare with James or Peter or others. This is done before the beloved disciple's important witness at the foot of the cross where he, like no other male disciple, actually sees the death of Jesus and understands its significance (19:35). The author prepares for this with the following description:

> When Jesus saw his mother, and the disciple whom he loved standing near, he said to his mother, "Woman, behold, your son!" Then he said to the disciple, "Behold your mother!" And from that hour the disciple took her to his own home (19:26–27).

The above words cannot be limited to simply a last command on Jesus' part that a favorite disciple continue the care of his mother; any interpretation must also keep in mind the role that the beloved disciple must play for the audience of the gospel. M. DeGoedt[32] has suggested that the words "Behold your mother" are a revelatory formula introducing a special new role as a mother that Mary will exercise in regard to the beloved disciple and his community. The author must establish a direct link with Jesus for the credentials of the beloved disciple as his most important witness. Consequently, a last word of Jesus confirming a relationship between his mother and the beloved disciple would be most significant. It would establish him as a "brother of the Lord" with authority like that of James, Jesus' blood relative, or other disciples of Jesus, even Peter.

R.E. Brown has written, "By stressing not only that his mother has become the mother of the beloved disciple, but also that the disciple has become her son, the Johannine Jesus is logically claiming the disciple as his true brother."[33] We thus arrive at another very important clue: *The relationship between the mother of Jesus and the beloved disciple is a very important one as guaranteeing the credibility and successorship of the beloved disciple to Jesus.* This clue will be pursued in a future chapter dealing with the relationship between these two principal witnesses of the death of Jesus and its meaning.

4
Key to a New Approach:
The Journey Structure of the Fourth Gospel

This chapter will argue that the fourth gospel has used the journey of Jacob in Genesis, chapters 28 to 35, as a literary and exegetical model[34] for the Johannine journey of the Word/Jesus. The results of such an approach, if conclusive, would shed important new light on the total meaning of the gospel as well as on the identity and role of Jesus' beloved disciple. We shall point out that this journey begins with the first disciples' call, culminating in that of Nathanael (1:45–51), and ends with Thomas' confession followed by Jesus' final blessing on those who do not see but believe (20:24–29) and a summary conclusion (20:30–31). We will also suggest that the Nathanael and Thomas stories form a literary bracket for the beginning and ending of this Johannine journey narrative.

In our literary approach, we will take our starting point from the text of the gospel as it now stands. In doing so, we are presuming that the final editor (if there was one) or author felt that it made sense in this form for the audience who would listen to his gospel. This does not mean that we do not consider the findings of source criticism to be valuable for understanding the process by which the fourth gospel came into existence.

First of all, we are led to investigate Jacob's journey as a model because Jesus alludes to Jacob's ladder/dream immediately before the marriage feast of Cana, the first gospel sign singled out by the author (2:11). Jesus announces to Nathanael,

29

Amen, amen, I say to you, you will see heaven opened, and
the angels of God ascending and descending upon the Son of
Man (1:51).

The question as to whether this verse belongs to an earlier or
later redaction of the gospels is not our concern here. This question is taken up in a study by J. Neyrey[35] who also brings out
important Jacob allusions in this verse and its context.

Looking at 1:51 cited above, we note that the author uses the
plural Greek "you" in this statement. This indicates that the
words are addressed to the audience/disciples who are to understand them in view of what follows in the gospel. The Cana wedding is clearly the first of a series of signs, since it ends with the
words, "This first of signs Jesus did at Cana in Galilee, and manifested his glory and his disciples believed in him" (2:11). The
"opening of heaven" in 1:51 replaces the similar expression in the
other gospels at Jesus' baptism. This suggests that the marriage
feast of Cana and succeeding signs will constitute this "opening of
heaven" through Jesus, the Son of Man and revealer of God's
secrets (1:18; 5:20). Moreover, the verb "opened" is in the Greek
perfect tense, indicating that an action has already begun and
remains in effect.

Jesus alone can reveal God because the "only begotten God
(or Son in some mss, with other variants) who is in the bosom of
the Father, he has made him known" (1:18). Since this is pre-
ceded by the words, "No one has ever seen God," this final statement leads us to expect that only Jesus brings the believer to "see
God" through contact with him. The gospel will trace this process
until Jesus will say to Philip at his final testament, "He who has
seen me has seen the Father" (14:9). We will later point out how
the literary Johannine journey comes to a fitting conclusion with
Thomas' inner vision of God in Christ as he confesses, "My Lord
and my God" (20:28).

Consequently, Jesus' introduction to the Cana sign through
the reference to Jacob's dream (1:51) suggests an investigation of
the journey of Jacob in Genesis 28–35 to determine the extent to

which it may have influenced the evangelist's literary pattern and meaning.

Why Would the Author Choose Jacob's Journey As a Gospel Pattern?

It would be helpful to know why Jacob's journey would especially interest the writer and his audience, given the unique nature of his gospel in comparison with the synoptics. These latter describe Jesus' journey from Galilee to Jerusalem followed by his suffering, death and resurrection. The gospel of John, however, concentrates more on Jesus' "inner" journey, that of the Logos into the world and its return to the Father. The opening gospel verses announce this as follows, "In the beginning was the Word and the Word was God . . . all things were made through him." This Word incarnates itself in Jesus: "And the word became flesh and dwelt among us" (1:12). At the end of Jesus' life, the incarnate Word returns to God. At the last supper, the writer notes, "Jesus, knowing that the Father had given all things into his hands, and that he had come from God and was going to God, rose from the supper" (13:1). In Jesus' last testament in chapters 14–16 he announces that he is returning to his "Father's house" (14:2) and describes how his disciples can also follow him there. In his final prayer, Jesus announces that he has completed his work on earth and asks the Father to glorify him with the glory he had with the Father before the world was made (17:5).

In John's gospel, we still have Jesus' journey to the cross and death. However, it appears to be more like the "external" part of the journey, while the real "inner" part is the journey of the Logos into this world and then its return to God. In John's gospel, the "external" journey, through the use of signs, is a way to enter into a relationship with the eternal Word acting in Jesus. Aptly then, Jesus describes himself as a *way* to the Father (14:4–6).

For a pattern of the Logos' journey, the author would likely have picked a familiar one to his audience. Already Philo of Alexandria had described Jacob's dream as an encounter with the divine Logos that would guide him on his journey.[36] However, the Greek Christian audience of the gospel would more likely have known the Greek book of Wisdom, in addition to other wisdom literature. J.-M. Braun[37] has illustrated how key wisdom themes on the fourth gospel are closely related to the wisdom biblical literature, especially that of the book of Wisdom.

In the book of Wisdom we find a description of Wisdom's journey through history. There she worked as an inner guide to the great figures of Hebrew history beginning from Adam and continuing to Moses (10:1–21). The work of Wisdom is similar to that of the Logos in the book of Wisdom. The author places them in parallel: "You have made all things by your word and by your wisdom you have formed human beings . . . " (9:1–2). Her (Wisdom's) work in Jacob, especially in his journey and dream, receives special attention:

> Wisdom rescued from troubles those who served her. When a righteous man fled from his brother's wrath, she guided him on straight paths; she showed him the kingdom of God, and gave him knowledge of angels (or holy things); she prospered him in his labors, and increased the fruit of his toil. When his oppressors were covetous, she stood by him and made him rich. She protected him from his enemies and kept him safe from those who lay in wait for him; in his arduous contest she gave him the victory, so that he might learn that godliness is more powerful than anything (Wis 10:9–12).

In the passage above, we note the special emphasis on Jacob's dream. There, "Wisdom showed him the kingdom of God and gave him knowledge of holy things" (10:10). C. Rowland[38] has studied how this early Hellenistic image of Jacob's reception of heavenly secrets is also prominent in Jewish apocalyptic and Targumic literature, showing that it was rather widespread. In the latter group, Jacob's dream and guidance are attributed to God's *Memra* or Word.

Another possible reason for the author's choice of the Jacob journey as a pattern may have been the "sign" character of that narrative, where the exterior events pointed to the inner working of the Logos/Wisdom. D. K. Clark[39] has illustrated how this sign character of Wisdom is an influence on the fourth gospel, but he did not mention Jacob's journey. A list of the signs during Jacob's journey is found in the Genesis narrative, the source of the above cited passage in Wisdom 10:9–12. For example, immediately after Jacob's dream/vision, he journeys quickly to Paddan-aram where he meets his future bride at a well and demonstrates enormous strength by moving a huge stone well cover that ordinarily required the concentrated effort of all the shepherds (29:10). This is a sign of the new inner strength he has received from God, and also a sign to Rachel his future bride. Later, Jacob is able to obtain property and inheritance despite Laban's trickery because the God of Bethel has intervened in his favor and confirmed this in another dream (31:11–13).

As time goes on, the marvels on Jacob's journey become more and more legendary. While the Targum of Jonathan is much later than John's gospel, it is an interesting witness of this continuing signs tradition. This Targum lists five "signs"[40] on Jacob's journey, beginning with Jacob's strength at the well, to which is added a miraculous overflow of the well during the twenty years that Jacob stayed with his uncle Laban.

If we could be sure that the extrabiblical document "The Ladder of Jacob" was circulated near the time of the composition of the fourth gospel, it would be an added indication of the popularity of the Jacob dream/journey motif. However, the evidence for such an early date of "The Ladder of Jacob" is very tenuous.[41]

Jacob's Dream—Parallels to the Johannine Journey of Jesus/Word

We begin by briefly sketching the context of Jacob's dream. Jesus' reference to the angels of God ascending and descending comes from the story of Jacob's dream/vision at Bethel (Gen 28:12). This took place during a great crisis in the life of Jacob/Israel. He had deceived both his father and his brother Esau by pretending that he was the first-born son and fraudulently obtaining his father's last blessing. In hatred and frustration, Esau planned to kill Jacob. To save his life, and to obtain a wife (and descendants to fulfill God's promises), his parents sent him away on a long difficult journey to Mesopotamia. Jacob was very much alone, in danger of his life, and fearful that he would not be able to find a wife and return to his home. On the way he stopped at a holy place, Bethel, either unknowingly or perhaps to pray for the success of his journey. An answer came from God in the form of an unusual dream (28:10–22) to which Jesus refers in his reply to Nathanael.

In the dream God reveals himself to Jacob through the vision of a ladder going up to heaven. The angels of God are ascending (with his prayers) and descending with God's response and gifts. God assures Jacob that he will be with him on his journey, and that he will have numerous descendants (hence he will find the wife) and return safely home. A central point is that Jacob/Israel sees the Lord at the top of the ladder (or perhaps beside him). This brings out a special privilege of Israel as one who has seen the Lord (see also 32:30 where Jacob says that he has seen God face to face). After the vision, Jacob goes safely on his journey and finds his future wives, Rachel and Leah. The happy ending of the first leg of the journey is their marriage feast (29:22), parallel to the marriage feast of Cana as the first stop in Jesus' journey.

The key words in the dream are God's promise and Jacob's response. God says to him, "The land on which you lie I will give to you and to your descendants" (28:13). Jacob replies with a vow,

If God will be with me and will keep me in this way that I go, and will give me bread to eat and clothing to wear, so that I come again to my father's house in peace, then the Lord shall be my God (28:20–21).

With this background of Jacob's journey/dream in mind, we can list some significant parallels to the Johannine journey narrative. First of all, we note immediately the closing words of Jacob's vow, "The Lord shall be my God." They seem like a counterpart to the confession of Thomas near the end of the gospel with the words, "My Lord and my God" (20:28).

Second, Jacob's vision contains the essential promise that God will accompany him on his journey. The heavens are opened so the angels as well as God can come down to him. God says, "Behold I am with you and will keep you wherever you go, and will not leave you until I have done that of which I have spoken to you" (28:15). With this assurance, Jacob concludes his vow with the words, "So that I may come again to my *father's house* in peace, and then the Lord shall be my God" (28:21). We note the similarity to the journey of the logos in the gospel and Jesus' return to his *father's house,* of which he speaks in his last testament to his disciples (14:1–2). Also, Jacob calls the place *Bethel,* "the house of God," and the "gate of heaven" (28:17). This gate or door corresponds to the "opening of the heavens" that Jesus promised to Nathanael (1:51). It is also linked to Jesus' description of himself as "the door" and as the way to the heavenly mansion (14:1–7, 8–10).

The end of Jacob's journey is also very similar to the end of the journey of Jesus/Logos in the fourth gospel. After a long delay, Jacob finally fulfills his vow to return to Bethel where "God had revealed himself to him" (35:8). God likewise has finished his journey with Jacob and returns to heaven: "God went up from him in the place where he had spoken with him" (35:14). The words used in the Greek Bible for "God went up" are *anēbē ho theos.* It is the same verb used by Jesus when he announces to Mary Magdalene, "I ascend (*anabainō*) to my Father and your Father, to my God and your God" (20:17). This ascension of God is especially emphasized by the Book of Jubilees in these words, "And he [God] finished speaking with him and went up from him, and Jacob watched until he went up to heaven."[42] In addition, the Targums, although later than John, seem to be making the biblical text more explicit. Thus the Targum of Jonathan has these words, "And the *Shekinah* of the Lord ascended from him in the place where he had spoken to him."[43] The Targum of Onqelos has the following, "And the glory of the Lord ascended above him in the place where he had spoken with him."[44]

This ascension logically takes place after Jesus' last words on earth to Thomas, immediately after he affirms that Jesus is God, *Theos* (20:28). Jesus then gives a final blessing that is especially addressed to the gospel audience: "Blessed are those who have not seen and yet believe" (20:29b). This corresponds to God's final blessing to Jacob before leaving him: "God appeared to Jacob again, when he came from Paddan-aram, and blessed him" (35:9). The blessing takes the form of a new name, Israel instead of Jacob. Keeping in mind the popular Jewish Hellenistic etymology of Israel as one who sees God (found forty times in Philo), the last blessing of Jacob in Genesis is similar to the theme of "seeing God" in Thomas' confession and Jesus' final blessing.

Third, the sign Jacob asked for in his vow would have been very significant for the gospel writer: "If God will . . . give me bread to eat" (28:20). This of course is a central sign of the gospel of John, where the bread that Jesus will give them to eat is mentioned some thirty times in chapter 6 with its sign of the loaves. The correct meaning of the bread that Jesus will give is so important that it causes serious division among his disciples. Some even leave him because of this teaching (6:41, 52, 60, 66).

Fourth, some important events during Jacob's journey also resemble parts of the journey of Jesus in John's gospel, and may have influenced the author's selection of stories. The motivation for Jacob's journey comes from his mother's plan to provide a wife and descendants for her son (Gen 27:43–44). As a result of God's accompanying presence promised in the dream, Jacob finally arrives at Haran at the end of a long, thousand mile journey. At Haran God gives Jacob a first sign in the form of a "water miracle." I call it a water miracle because the watering of Rachel's sheep is mentioned five times in the story as a result of Jacob's sudden and unexpected strength in removing the enormous stone from the top of the well (29:1–10). No doubt the event receives such attention from the writer because it is God's "arrangement" for the formative marriage that results in the people of Israel.

After witnessing this "miracle," Rachel, Jacob's future bride, runs to tell her father Laban who welcomes him into his home. A month afterward Jacob agrees to work seven years to obtain

Rachel as his wife. The wedding feast, *gamos*, LXX, with its free-flowing wine, marks the end of this time (29:22). This marriage feast and the birth of children from both Rachel and Leah mark the success of the first part of Jacob's journey. In parallel, the first gospel sign after Jesus' reference to Jacob's ladder is the marriage feast, *gamos*, at Cana, with its sign of water changed to wine (2:1–12).

In addition, just as Jacob met Rachel at a well, so also Jesus meets the Samaritan woman at a well in Samaria which is called the well of Jacob (Jn 4:1–6). In both stories there is specific mention of the journey motif. Jacob leaves Bethel, journeys to Haran and finds the well; Jesus, tired from his journey, arrives in Samaria where he sits down beside the well. To strengthen the connection to Jacob, the evangelist notes that this was near the field that Jacob gave to his son Joseph (4:5). This was the first place where Jacob arrived on his return to Israel and where he bought a plot of ground (Gen 33:18). In the dialogue between Jesus and the Samaritan woman, she asks him, "Are you greater than our father Jacob, who gave us the well, and drank from it himself, and his sons, and his cattle?" (4:12). These and other allusions to the Jacob tradition are brought out in another study by J. Neyrey.[45]

Fifth, the concluding "memorial" at the end of each journey is similar. At the end of Jacob's last vision, he erects a pillar in memorial of the events (35:14). This may co-relate to the final notice and "memorial" of the writer or beloved disciple: "these things are written that you may believe" (20:31). There is an early confirmation of the writing on Jacob's pillar at Bethel in the Book of Jubilees which has the following: "He [Jacob] woke up from his sleep and recalled everything that he had read and seen and he wrote down all the matters which he had read and seen."[46] These words refer to the Book of Jubilees' account of Jacob's vision in a dream of seven tablets on which were written all that would happen to him and his sons.

Sixth, the "seeing of God" motif is quite evident in both journeys. During his dream/journey, Jacob's visions of God are high points. First he sees the Lord by the ladder (28:13); then after the wrestling with an angel, he calls the place Penuel, saying, "I have seen God face to face, and yet my life is preserved" (32:30). Later Jewish writings, avoiding such direct language in meetings with the deity, referred to Jacob as seeing the "glory of God." This language is used by the Targums to describe these encounters. While later than John's gospel they reflect a growing tendency to avoid direct mention of God. Thus the fourth gospel frequently uses the word "glory" for such encounters with the deity. The signs of Jesus in this gospel are ways of experiencing the "glory of God" manifested in Jesus (2:11; 11:4, 40). The total experience is summed up in the words, "We saw his glory, glory as of the only Son from the Father" (1:14).

Seventh, the occurrence of the "twin" motif in the Jacob cycle as well as in the Jesus' story is also quite unusual. The only twins in the Bible are in Jacob's family and Thomas in the gospels. Only John seems to emphasize the fact in 11:16; 20:24; 21:2. Jacob, of course, and Esau are twins (*thomim,* Hebr., or *didyma,* LXX [Gen 25:24]). They also seem to run in the family (38:27)! Jacob "loses" Esau but God in effect gives him a new name and mission when Jacob returns to Bethel: "No longer shall your name be called Jacob but Israel shall be your name" (35:10). This change of name also appears in another story where Jacob wrestles with a mysterious being and receives the name Israel based on the etymology of one who has struggled with God and won (32:28). The text also brings out that Israel has seen God's face at this time, since Jacob calls the name of the place Peniel, saying, "I have seen God face to face and yet my life is preserved" (32:30). As already noted, in the Jewish Hellenistic world the name Israel was connected with seeing God, although not really based on its true etymology.

In parallel to the Genesis story, Thomas, the New Testament twin, becomes a "twin" of Israel by seeing God in Christ through his confession, "My Lord and my God." This seems to be a counterpart of Jacob's vow: "Then the Lord shall be my God" (28:21). Since Thomas' confession comes from a revelation, like that of Jacob, it also amounts to a corresponding "opening of the heavens" that prepares the way for Jesus' ascension to the Father. The double reference to the closed doors when Jesus came to his disciples (20:19, 26) may be a symbolic contrast to Jesus' role as the "door" to the Father (10:9).

Eight and last: Perhaps the most important link between the Jacob and Jesus journeys is the common Bethel/temple theme at the beginning and end of each. The following descriptions suggest this: the Jacob journey begins mysteriously with his arrival "at a certain place" (28:10). On awakening from his significant dream, Jacob exclaims, "Surely the Lord was in this place and I did not know it." In view of this divine presence, Jacob calls the place "Bethel, *the house of God*" (28:17). Consequently, Jacob vows to build there a place of worship. He promises, "This stone which I have set up for a pillar shall be God's house," and adds that he will financially support worship there by saying, "Of all you give me, I will give you tithes" (28:22).

At the end of Jacob's journey, God himself gave him the final order to return to Bethel to offer worship. He said to him, "Arise, go up to Bethel, and dwell there; and make an altar to the God who appeared to you when you fled from your brother Esau" (35:1). In obedience to God, and to fulfill his vow, Jacob returns to Bethel where he offers worship by setting up a sacred pillar and pouring drink offerings upon it (35:15). Once again he names the place "Bethel, *the house of God.*" Thus both the journey of Jacob and the inner journey of the Word/Wisdom in Jacob begin and end at Bethel, where God "goes up" to heaven just as Jacob "goes up" to Bethel (35:1,13).

The temple motif in Jacob's journey is also very evident in early extrabiblical literature where it may be connected to the hope that God will build a future temple in the last times. The Book of Jubilees dwells at length on Jacob's worship at Bethel and his intention to build a temple there. Jubilees has Jacob fulfill his promise to worship on that spot by describing how this took place at the feast of Tabernacles with Levi the priest offering sacrifices at Bethel.[47] Jacob also desired to build a temple in the same place: "Jacob planned to build up that place and to build a wall around the court and to sanctify it and to make it eternally holy for himself and his sons after him."[48] However, Jacob had a dream and vision in which he saw an angel descend with seven tablets on which it was described what would happen in future ages. God told Jacob, "Do not build this place, and do not make an eternal sanctuary here because this is not the place."[49] J. Schwartz[50] has suggested that Jubilees' special concentration on Jacob's desire to build a Bethel temple may be due to cultic tension between Jerusalem and Bethel in the late second century B.C.

The temple scroll of the Dead Sea Scrolls continues the emphasis on the connections between Jacob, the temple and Bethel in these words of God,

> I will consecrate my Temple by my glory on which I will settle my glory until the day of the blessing [or, in the day of creation] on which I will create my Temple and establish it for myself for all times according to the covenant which I have made with Jacob at Bethel.[51]

By way of comparison, we can now suggest that the journey of the Word in John's gospel begins and ends with the same temple theme, based on the model of the Jacob/Bethel journey. The fourth gospel begins with the summary prologue statement that Jesus became a temple of the Word: "The Word became flesh and pitched his tent among us" (1:14). These words announce a journey motif. Yet Jesus' disciples will only know Jesus as the temple of the Word after his resurrection.

This post-resurrection knowledge is indicated by the writer immediately after the wedding at Cana in the story of Jesus' visit to Jerusalem and cleansing of the temple. The emphasis in the account is on the *Father's house* and on fulfilling the scriptures, "Zeal for your *house* will consume me" (2:17). When the Jews ask Jesus for a supporting sign, he replies, "Destroy this temple and in three days I will raise it up" (2:16–19). The Jews do not understand Jesus' answer, so the writer makes the significant remark:

> But he spoke of the temple of his body. When therefore he was raised from the dead, his disciples remembered that he had said this; and they believed the scripture and the word which Jesus had spoken (2:22–23).

In view of this body of Jesus/temple theme, the journey of the Word begins after Jesus selects his disciple/companions for the journey. The selection of the last, Nathanael, has special significance since it is followed by Jesus' announcement of Jacob's ladder at Bethel and the angels of God ascending and descending upon the Son of Man (1:51). Philip finds Nathanael and announces that he has found the one of whom Moses and the prophets had spoken. When Nathanael expresses his disbelief, Philip invites him to see for himself by replying, "Come and see" (1:46). Nathanael responds to the invitation and comes to see Jesus.

Jesus' words to the disciples/gospel audience upon seeing Nathanael come are very significant: "Behold a true Israelite in whom there is no guile" (1:47). We have already suggested that these words prepare for a central Johannine theme; that to come to Jesus and see him is to come to see the Father and that this all leads up to Thomas seeing Jesus and confessing him as his Lord and God. However, to avoid confusion we did not then suggest a possible underlying temple theme.

This temple theme is based on the common perception of the Israelite that coming to Jerusalem to worship is coming to "see God." This idea is especially found in the worship context of the psalms. For example, the worshiper expresses a most intense desire to dwell in the house of the Lord all the days of life "to behold the beauty of the Lord" (27:4). Likewise, the pilgrim prays, "My soul thirsts for God. . . . When shall I come and behold the face of God" (42:2). Again, "I have looked upon you in the sanctuary, beholding your power and glory" (63:2). Finally, "the God of gods will be seen in Zion" (84:7).

In the above texts we note the emphasis on *seeing*. This emphasis begins in the prologue statement, "We have *seen* his glory, glory as of the only begotten from the Father" (1:14). This seeing becomes possible since Jesus dwells in the bosom of the Father and sees him, thus making it possible to reveal the Father to others even though no one thus far has seen God (1:18). This seeing motif is found in Nathanael's call; he is invited by Philip to "come and see" (1:46). Jesus tells him that a greater *seeing* will take place than Jesus' previous knowledge of Nathanael under the fig tree. Jesus then refers to Jacob's vision at Bethel by telling him (and the disciples/audience) that they will *see* the angels of God ascending and descending on the Son of Man. This temple/house of God theme at Bethel invites us to look further to see if Jesus will lead his disciples to a "seeing of God" similar to that of Jacob.

Especially within the resurrection stories, the writer seems to be carefully preparing for the final confession of Thomas. There seems to be a gradual crescendo both in the use of the verb "to see" and the title "Lord." Mary reports to the disciples, "I have *seen* the Lord" (20:18). Then Jesus appears to the assembled group and "the disciples were glad when they *saw* the Lord" (20:20). Next the disciples tell Thomas, "We have *seen* the Lord" (20:24). Thomas, however, replies, "Unless I *see* in his hands . . . I will not believe" (20:25). Finally Thomas does see Jesus and exclaims, "My Lord and my God" (20:28). These words of Thomas are not just a credal statement but an act of worship using words addressed to God in Psalm 35:23. They do not result from the mere sight of Jesus' body which Thomas could identify by seeing and touching the wounds. They come from recognizing Jesus' body as a temple, and seeing God in him in the same way that pilgrims came to worship at the temple and "saw God."

Consequently, Jesus' journey seems parallel to the Jacob journey which began at Bethel, house of God, and ended with worship at the same spot. Accessory final elements may be the closed doors when Jesus appeared to the disciples and later to Thomas (20:19, 26). This would contrast with Christ the door (10:7) and the "door of heaven" at Bethel (Gen 28:17). In addition, the reference to the disciples being "inside" (20:26) may have a double meaning: the worship of Jesus in the house makes it truly a house of God, another Bethel.

With the above closing in mind, the words of Jesus to his disciples/gospel audience may have special additional meaning: "Behold a true Israelite in whom there is no guile"(1:47). To be "without guile" is among the qualifications for seeing God and dwelling in his holy temple that are expressed in Psalms 15:1–3 and 24:3–4 where the psalmist answers the question, "Who shall sojourn in your tent? Who shall dwell on your holy hill?" Thus this description paves the way for the theme of Jesus as God's holy temple that will be brought out in the subsequent journey.

Nathanael–Bethel/Temple–Thomas: Beginning and Ending

With the above background, we can examine more closely the relationship between Nathanael, Israel and Thomas. Jesus introduces Nathanael to his disciples/gospel audience with the words, "Behold a true Israelite in whom there is no guile" (1:47). Since Jesus says these words while he sees Nathanael coming toward him, R.E. Brown[52] notes that the author is describing a true Israelite as one who comes to Jesus, an idea expressed elsewhere in the gospel. Jesus promises Nathanael (and the disciples) a further "seeing," parallel to that of Jacob/Israel, by saying, "You shall see greater things than these" (1:50). Finally, Thomas plays a true twin role to that of Nathanael by actually seeing the Lord in Jesus and exclaiming "My Lord and my God" (20:28). It is fitting, then, that the so-called gospel "appendix" names Thomas and Nathanael side by side in its opening verse (21:1).

With the above general parallels in mind, we can now make a more detailed comparison between Nathanael and Thomas. This, we believe, will show that we have a literary bracket marking the beginning and end of a journey narrative within the fourth gospel.

1. Jesus directly calls Philip, who then tells Nathanael, *"We have found* him of whom Moses in the law and also the prophets wrote, Jesus of Nazareth, the son of Joseph" (1:45). Nathanael refuses to believe this and hints that he must see for himself; he says, "Can anything good come out of Nazareth?" Philip replies to him, "Come and *see"* (1:45–46). Nathanael responds to this invitation.

In counterpart, "Thomas, one of the twelve, called the Twin, was not with them when Jesus came. So the other disciples told him, *'We have seen* the Lord' " (20:24). Like Nathanael, Thomas refuses the witness of others and demands physical proof: "Unless I see in his hands the print of the nails, and place my finger in the mark of the nails, and place my hand in his side, I will not believe" (20:25). Again, like Nathanael, he does come to Jesus by being present at the next disciples' gathering.

2. Jesus gives Nathanael a sign by telling him that even before they met he had seen him sitting under a fig tree (1:48). In parallel, Jesus appears to Thomas and invites him to see his wounds with his own eyes and put his fingers in them (20–27). In both cases, there is evidence of special knowledge usually attributed to God; in the second case, Jesus mysteriously knew Thomas' previous reaction to the disciples' witness.

3. Both then make a profession of faith. Nathanael exclaims, "Rabbi, you are the Son of God! You are the king of Israel." Thomas says, "My Lord and my God." With the Jacob story background, the parallels become even closer in the words of Jacob, "The Lord will be my God" (Gen 28:21). "Son of God" and "king of Israel" actually conform to the concluding statement about the signs worked by Jesus so that the audience may believe that he is Christ (equivalent to "king of Israel") and "Son of God" (20:31)—but now in a deeper sense than the words of Nathanael.

4. The concluding statement of Jesus in both episodes is an invitation to go beyond the sign or miracle to a deeper faith based on an inner seeing of Jesus and not external sight. Jesus tells Nathanael, "*Because I saw* you under the fig tree, *do you believe?* You shall see greater things than these. Amen I say to you, you shall see heaven opened and the angels of God ascending and descending upon the Son of Man" (1:50–51). As a twin ending, Jesus says to Thomas, "*Have you believed because you have seen me?* Blessed are those who have not seen and yet believe" (20:29). R. Fortna has suggested that this is a fitting ending to the Thomas story as a blessing is pronounced on the later audience of the gospel.

5. It should also be added that the revelation to Thomas, as the literary twin to Nathanael, also completes a way or journey that begins with 1:43 where Jesus decides to go to Galilee and calls his first disciples. The announcement of Jacob's dream of the descending and ascending angels also parallels the beginning of the journey of the Word with Jacob. God tells him that he will be with him on his *way* and Jacob promises to keep a vow if God

keeps him on his *way, hodos* in the LXX (28:20). Angels meet Jacob on his *way* (32:1). In parallel, Jesus as *way* is emphasized in 14:4–6, where he says to *Thomas,* "I am the way." This will only become evident to Thomas at Jesus' last apparition when he recognizes him as the Lord just before Jesus presumably returns to his Father. In parallel, Jacob/Israel at the return of his journey puts aside all foreign gods and keeps his promise that the Lord will be his God (35:1–15). The experience of Nathanael is the gateway, paralleled by Jacob's experience at Bethel, which he calls the "gate of heaven" (28:17). The twin ending of the journey is the revelation to Thomas that Jesus is indeed the manifestation of the Father and the "door" or "way" to God (Jn 20:28).

The unusual correspondences between beginning and end in the stories of Nathanael and Thomas, I believe, are sufficient to argue that we have the conclusion of a journey narrative in 20:31 corresponding to an opening in 1:51 with Jacob's new ladder as the revelatory Son of Man. This revelation starts in the following signs, beginning with the first, the marriage feast of Cana.

Conclusion

The Jewish Hellenistic image of Wisdom accompanying Jacob on his journey and enlightening him in his dream leads us to investigate whether the fourth gospel has used Jacob's journey as a literary and exegetical pattern. Jesus' own direct reference to Jacob's dream preceding the marriage feast at Cana points in this direction. Samples of significant parallels and areas of influence are the following: Jacob's vow: "If God will be with me . . . and will give me bread to eat . . . so that I come again to my father's house in peace . . . then the Lord will be my God" (Gen 28:20). Likewise, Thomas' confession, "My Lord and my God," occurs before Jesus' last words and his return to his Father's house (14:2; 20:28–29). For Jacob, the heavens are opened and God comes down to be with him on his journey; on his return, God went up (*anēbē*) in 35:13, just as Jesus says "I ascend," *anabainō* (20:17). Especially important is the parallel Bethel/temple building theme in Jacob's journey and that of the Logos. In addition, a comparison between Nathanael and Thomas indicates that they form a literary *inclusio* at the beginning and ending of the Johannine journey narrative.

Consequences for Our Search for
the Identity of the Beloved Disciple

The literary parallels between the journey of Jacob with his twelve sons/successors and Jesus and his twelve disciples/ successors provide a valuable framework for discovering the identity and role of Jesus' beloved disciple. In our next chapter, we will argue that the fourth gospel is building on the parallel of Joseph as beloved son and successor of Jacob.

5

The Beloved Disciple as Jesus'
Successor and Son, Modeled on Joseph,
Beloved Son and Successor of Jacob

In our last chapter, we presented Jacob's journey as a literary model for the journey of the Word/Jesus in the fourth gospel. Our next step is to examine this pattern more closely. As we do so we will find another remarkable similarity. The journey of Jacob centers about the theme of succession: Jacob's marriage makes possible the birth of his sons who eventually become the twelve tribes of Israel/Jacob. Among these twelve, the continued narrative centers on Joseph, the beloved son of Jacob. Joseph is the chosen instrument to insure the future of the others by rescuing them from hunger by bringing them into Egypt where they can have bread and life.

First of all, let us examine the succession theme. The journey of Jacob concludes with his visit to Bethel to fulfill his vow. After that the narrative prepares the way for the future by noting, "The sons of Jacob were twelve" (Gen 35:22). Then they are all listed by name. After the death of Isaac, Jacob's father, there follows a genealogy of his descendants. Then the next journey of Jacob's descendants begins, a journey which centers about Joseph in chapters 37 to 50. The writer starts this with the note, "This is the history of the family of Jacob" (37:2) and then proceeds to tell his audience about Joseph, beginning from his youth in his father's house.

The book of Genesis comes to a climactic point with the deathbed scene of Jacob, the patriarch and father of the twelve tribes. He makes his final testament and gives his last blessing to each of his sons who must carry on after him. Among the sons, Joseph is singled out for the most attention as well as an unusual abundance of blessings. In fact, the word "blessing" is not even used of the others, but used seven times[53] in 49:25–26 as if to suggest that Joseph receives a sevenfold or fullness of blessing. Even before the final blessing, this special place of Joseph is brought out through Jacob's unusual gift to Joseph of a mountain slope that Jacob acquired through a victory over the Amorites. Jacob says to Joseph, "I have given to you *rather than to your brothers* one mountain slope which I took from the hand of the Amorites with my sword and with my bow" (48:22).

The preeminence of Joseph is further confirmed by the fact that Jacob adopts the two sons of Joseph, Ephraim, and Manasseh, as his very own. The story is told in great detail (Gen 48:1–22). Jacob declares that his two grandsons will be his own just as Reuben and Simeon. He has the boys brought up to him and places them on his knees in a ritual of adoption. He kisses and embraces them, then places his hands on the head of each to give them a special blessing. This means in effect that Joseph will have a double inheritance among the sons of Jacob and tribes of Israel.

The final blessing and testament of Moses in Deuteronomy also witnesses the special inheritance of Joseph. It starts with the words, "This is the blessing with which Moses the man of God blessed the children of Israel before his death" (Dt 33:1). Yet of all the sons of Jacob, Moses singles out Joseph for the greatest and longest praise, and actually uses the word "blessing" only of him with the words, "Blessed by the Lord be his land" (33:13). He is also called "prince among his brothers" (33:16).

Second, the reason for Joseph's primacy will be especially important for us. It is because he is the beloved son of Jacob, as the offspring of his special love for Rachel. The author of Genesis notes:

> Now Israel loved Joseph more than any other of his children, because he was the son of his old age, and he made him a long robe with sleeves. But when his brothers saw that their father loved him more than all his brothers, they hated him (37:3–40).

In addition to this special love, Joseph is also described as being closer to God than the other brothers. He is gifted with God's secrets through dreams and divine revelations from God. One of these is the means for saving the whole land of Egypt, and later the sons of Israel from hunger and starvation (chapter 41 on Pharaoh's dream). It is often repeated that the Lord was with Joseph and gave him special favor (39:2, 4, 21, 23). The author, through the mouth of Pharaoh, praises Joseph with the words, "Can we find such a man as this, in whom is the Spirit of God?" (41:38).

In extrabiblical literature, we find the same emphasis on Joseph as beloved son and successor of Jacob. In the Testament of the Twelve Patriarchs,[54] we have these words in the Testament of Joseph: "Listen to Joseph, the one beloved of Israel" (1:2). Also, "For my brothers know how much my father loved me" (10:5).

Putting together what we have now found about Jacob's journey as a literary pattern for the journey of Jesus/Word in the fourth gospel, as well as the unusual place of Joseph as special successor and beloved son of Israel, we can see that the author of our gospel could have found in the Old Testament a remarkable pattern for his presentation of the beloved disciple as successor of Jesus. We shall also see that the beloved disciple fits very well the image of an adopted son of Jesus. We must then turn to the gospel itself to verify whether the author does in fact follow such a pattern.

Before we do turn to the gospel, we should note that P. Minear[55] has broken the ground for looking to the Old Testament for an understanding of the role and identity of the beloved disciple. Minear has made a special point that Benjamin is called the "beloved of the Lord" in Moses' last testament in Deuteronomy 33:12. However, this is because Benjamin's land is close to where the temple will be built, and thus his blessing follows that of Levi which is emphasized because of his temple priesthood. In addition to this, there are a number of other ways[56] that Benjamin would not fit as a model for the beloved disciple.

The Disciple at the Lord's Bosom: Adopted Son and Successor of Jesus on the Model of Joseph, Beloved Son and Successor of Jacob

First of all, the author's interest in Joseph would certainly follow from his detailed use of the journey of Jacob and his twelve successors as a model. The writer was surely aware that Joseph was Jacob's beloved son and special successor. In addition, the gospel has a specific reference to this unique place of Joseph: "He [Jesus] came to a city of Samaria, called Sychar, near the field that Jacob gave to his son Joseph" (4:5). This is a reference to the text we have already quoted from Genesis 28:42 where this land was given to Joseph as a special portion *more than his brothers*.

Here, however, we wish to argue from the text of the fourth gospel that the references to the beloved disciple do in fact point to his role as a successor and "son" almost independently of the background of Joseph in Jacob's journey. Yet if we put both together, the image of the beloved disciple in those roles is confirmed for the gospel audience.

The Disciple at the Bosom of Jesus

First of all, in the Bible, to be in someone's bosom describes the most intimate of all human relationships. It is used of a husband or wife (e.g. Gen 16:5; Dt 13:6; 28:54, 56). However, this closeness is especially true of a child in regard to father or mother (e.g. 2 Sam 12:3; 1 Kgs 3:20; 17:19). It has also the connotation of a special place where secrets are kept (Job 31:33; Ps 89:50; Eccl 7:9). The familiar picture of Lazarus at the messianic banquet in the bosom of Abraham indicates the height of privileged sonship (Lk 16:22, 23). For our purposes, the ceremony of adoption by taking another's child into the bosom may be significant in examining the significance of the image of the beloved disciple in Jesus' bosom (cf. Ru 4:16–17 where Naomi adopts Ruth's son by taking him into her bosom and making him her heir as well).

However, the essential matter is to discover the meaning of this phrase within the context of John, chapter 13. This chapter is part of a whole sequence, chapters 13–17, that forms Jesus' last words and testament before his coming departure and death. It begins with a reference to his death, as the author notes that Jesus knew his hour had come to depart from this world (13:1). It is a final meal of Jesus and his disciples. He washes their feet and tells them that they in the future must perform the same action for others: "I have given you an example, that you also should do as I have done to you." The disciples will carry on Jesus' work to such an extent that those who receive them will receive Jesus himself: "He who receives any one whom I send receives me" (13:20).

During this final meal, Jesus' last discourse and instructions to his disciples takes place in chapters 14–17. Central in these chapters is the theme that, although Jesus is going away, he and the Father will send to them a successor, the Paraclete, who will duplicate and continue the presence of Jesus among his disciples (14:25–28; 15:26–27; 16:7–15). This emphasis on continuity and succession is so important that Jesus prays not only for his disciples but for future believers converted through his successors: "I do not pray for these only but also for those who believe in me through their word" (17:20).

Consequently, it is supremely important that the beloved disciple first appears designated at this time as the disciple "whom Jesus loved" (13:23). He has a special place at the side of Jesus during his last will and testament to his disciples. Through this, the writer wishes to show that the beloved disciple is a most important heir of Jesus. This will be shown by the interchange between Jesus, this disciple and Peter during the supper.

Jesus carries within him the great secret that Judas, one of the twelve, is about to betray him. This matter is so crucial that it will set off the events leading to Jesus' saving death. This secret comes to the surface when the betrayer leaves the supper room under the control of Satan, and Jesus exclaims, "Now is the Son of Man glorified" (13:31). When Jesus, "troubled in spirit," announces that one of them is about to betray him, the disciples looked at one another, not knowing of whom he spoke (13:22). At this point, Simon Peter beckons to the beloved disciple lying at the bosom (*kolpos*) of Jesus and requests him to ask the master who it is (13:24). The disciple then leans on the chest (*stēthos*) of Jesus and finds out how the betrayer is to be identified by Peter.

We note in this last statement that Jesus' greatest secret is given first to the beloved disciple. Even Peter the rock must request it through him. There is a parallel to this in the resurrection apparitions of chapter 21, possibly an added appendix of the gospel. In the miraculous draught of fish, only the beloved disciple identifies the risen Jesus standing on the shore. He tells Peter that it is the Lord, and Peter depends on *hearing* this from the beloved disciple and jumps into the water (21:7). Thus we see that "lying at the bosom of Jesus" at the last supper, besides picturing an intimate relationship, has also the important meaning of sharing Jesus' greatest secret and revealing it to others, even Peter.

From this, we can move to further investigate the nature of the beloved disciple's relationship to Jesus. The gospel descriptions envision a father-son type relationship modeled on that between Jesus and his own Father. First of all, there is a striking parallel in the beginning of the gospel. There Jesus is described as the only son dwelling in the bosom of the Father who makes him known to others: "No one has ever seen God; the only Son, who is in the bosom of the Father, he has made him known" (1:18). The same revelation theme is also brought out in Jesus' statement, "The Father loves the Son and shows him all that he is doing" (5:20). Thus we have the combination of beloved son and revelation in Jesus' relationship to the Father (cf. also 8:28; 14:10). Putting it all together we would have the succession: God the Father–beloved son Jesus–beloved disciple and son.

All of this is confirmed by Jesus' final testament on the cross to his own mother and to the beloved disciple. He tells her, "Woman, behold your son." Then he tells the disciple whom he loved, "Behold your mother" (19:26–27). The immediate context of this statement is before the final events of Jesus' death which will be followed by an unusual flow of blood and water from the side of Jesus. The beloved disciple is a witness to this (no other male disciple is mentioned as present). The evangelist attaches special importance to this witness: "He who saw it has borne witness—his witness is true, and he knows that he tells the truth—that you also may believe (19:35). Thus the beloved disciple is the chosen person to make known the meaning of Jesus' death to others. His witness is guaranteed by his position as favorite son and successor of Jesus, a place sealed by Jesus' final words entrusting the beloved disciple to his own mother as a son. Thus the sonship relationship was continued on through the person most closely associated to Jesus, his own mother. This relationship and its significance will be further studied in chapter 8.

The Beloved Disciple as "Inner" Successor of Jesus

This thesis may be best illustrated through comparison with Peter. There is no question about the important place of Peter in this gospel. He is singled out in the beginning when Jesus meets him, looks upon him and gives him a new name in view of his special mission: "So you are Simon, son of John? You shall be called Cephas (which means Peter)" (1:42). It is Peter who makes a confession of faith for the others when many disciples leave Jesus because of his difficult saying about "eating his flesh" (6:66–68). On Easter morning, although the beloved disciple precedes Peter to the empty tomb, he does not enter first, but defers to Peter. After the resurrection, Jesus announces to Peter that he will continue his own shepherding role in regard to future believers (21:15–17). Peter's role seems to be more that of external successor as leader of the twelve.

In contrast, the beloved disciple has more of an inner, understanding role. At the last supper, he is the first to know Jesus' greatest secret about his betrayal and coming death. He witnesses Jesus' death on the cross and points to the special scriptural meaning of the flow of watery blood from his side (19:34–35). At the empty tomb he looks at the linen cloths and believes, whereas Peter does not seem to as yet understand that Jesus has risen

(20:8–10). In the resurrection apparition, 21:7, it is the beloved disciple who recognizes the risen Lord, and Peter relies on hearing this from him.

This inner witness and succession of the beloved disciple is especially evident in the story of what seems to be his own call by Jesus (1:35–40). Although only Andrew is named as one of the two disciples, there are good reasons to believe that the beloved disciple was the other: The story contains Jesus' first words to disciples, and thus parallel his very last words to the beloved disciple at the foot of the cross in 19:27. The account is also in much greater detail than the others, and seems to draw its source from personal reminiscences. Even the hour of the meeting is recalled (1:39).

In addition, the above encounter occurs after John the Baptist had pointed out Jesus as the "Lamb of God who takes away the sins of the world" (1:29). Thus it parallels the witness of the beloved disciple at Jesus' death that the unusual events point to Jesus' fulfillment of the scriptures about the eating of the paschal lamb and the sacrificial (flow of blood) nature of Jesus' death (19:34–37).

If this is indeed the call of the beloved disciple the details would appear to be especially meaningful in terms of his inner witness and mission:

> Jesus turned, and saw them following, and said to them, "What do you seek?" And they said to him, "Rabbi (which means Teacher), where are you staying?" He said to them, "Come and see." And they came and saw where he was staying; and they stayed with him that day, for it was about the tenth hour (1:37–39).

A number of significant points can be drawn from this account. If it is indeed the tenth hour, perhaps four o'clock, the disciples may very well have stayed with Jesus overnight in his temporary home. This is a special act of hospitality that could symbolize taking them into his own home or family. For the beloved disciple, it may have been the beginning of a relationship of adoption as a favorite son of Jesus. Secondly, there is special emphasis on the word "stay" or "abide" which is mentioned three times. This word "abide" has central importance in John's gospel. John the Baptist had been told that a special sign for him would be the descent of the Spirit on Jesus in the form of a dove and *abiding* on him. It would show the Baptist that Jesus is the one who baptizes with the Holy Spirit (1:32–34). Now Jesus with this abiding Spirit calls his disciples who abide with him, share his home. This may signify that they also share, or will share, the same abiding Spirit.

The Beloved Disciple and the Holy Spirit, the Paraclete[57]

If the beloved disciple is an inner successor of Jesus in terms of divine presence and understanding of his mission, how does this relate to the texts about the Spirit in John 14–16 who is described as "another Paraclete," one who would be a successor of Jesus after his death? If we look at the texts describing the role of the Paraclete, we will find the same descriptions of the role that the beloved disciple claims in the gospel. The Paraclete is the Spirit of truth (14:15); the beloved disciple also proclaims the truth (19:35). The Paraclete bears witness, as does the beloved disciple (15:26; 19:35). They both teach and bring into remembrance what Jesus has said (14:25; 2:20–22). Thus the beloved disciple especially exemplifies the inner work of the Paraclete.

We may summarize by putting together the clues from this chapter. *The beloved disciple has a role among Jesus' disciples similar to that held by Joseph among the sons of Israel. While Judah held the external role of supremacy among the twelve tribes, so also Peter held the role of external authority among Jesus' disciples. As Joseph was gifted as Jacob's beloved son and successor, so also the beloved disciple is an inner successor and favorite son of Jesus especially in matters of inner understanding. In this way, he is a living example of the working of the Holy Spirit which is the total inner successor of Jesus after his death. The story of the call of the beloved disciple also suggests a time where Jesus could have adopted him as a son.*

6
The Priestly Connection
and Its Significance

The evangelist tells us that the beloved disciple was known to the high priest and his household. When Jesus was brought into the courtyard of the high priest, Peter was not able to enter. But the "other disciple" (a designation of the beloved disciple also in 20:2) "was known to the high priest" (18:15) and entered the courtyard with Jesus. This is more than a casual acquaintance, for the phrase is repeated again in the next verse, and he is so well known that he can speak to the maid at the gate and use his influence to let Peter in. The indications above are brief, but they lead us to look in the area of possible family relationship—that the beloved disciple may have been a relative or member of a priestly family, as was his first mentor John the Baptist if we accept the evidence from Luke 1:5. It would also make it probable that the beloved disciple was from Judea, possibly Jerusalem, or that he visited there often enough to be well known at the high priest's household, which was indeed a distinguished one.

We would not be surprised, then, to find that the gospel, with its close connection to the beloved disciple, is especially interested in the priesthood and its significance. This special interest shows up in the meeting of chief priests and Pharisees after the resurrection of Lazarus. On this occasion, the group was concerned lest everyone might believe in Jesus, and that the Romans would come to destroy both the holy place and nation (11:48). The author then makes the following important statement:

But one of them, Caiaphas, who was high priest that year, said
to them, "You do not understand that it is expedient for you
that one man should die for the people, and that the whole
nation should not perish." He did not say this of his own
accord, but being high priest that year he prophesied that
Jesus should die for the nation, and not for the nation only,
but to gather into one the children of God who are scattered
abroad (11:49–51).

We note the sacrificial terminology of the "prophetic" statement of the high priest: "that one man should die for the people,"
and its interpretation by the evangelist in regard to the effects of
Jesus' death. The Old Testament descriptions of sacrifice en-
lighten the meaning of the high priest's statement. Leviticus, the
great "liturgical book," uses the term "for the people" in a sacrificial sense regarding atonement for sins: Moses said to Aaron,
"Draw near to the altar, and offer your sin offering and your
burnt offering, and make atonement for yourself and *for the people*" (9:7; cf. also 9:15, 18). The connection to forgiveness of sin is
especially brought out in the sacrifices on the day of atonement:

> Then he (the priest) shall kill the goat of the sin offering which
> is *for the people* and bring its blood within the veil, and do
> with its blood as he did with the blood of the bull, sprinkling it
> upon the mercy seat and before the mercy seat; thus he shall
> make atonement for the holy place, because of the unclean-
> nesses of the people of Israel, and because of their transgres-
> sions, all their sins (16:15–16).

Perhaps by way of irony, the author highlights the instrumen-
tality of the high priests in Jesus' death, for they are the very ones
who offer the sacrifices in the name of the people. Caiaphas first
proposes the idea, to which, as we have seen, the writer attaches
great significance (11:49–52). Later the author recalls this when
Jesus is brought to Caiaphas for examination: "It was Caiaphas
who had given counsel to the Jews that it was expedient that one
man should die for the people" (18:14). Pilate himself says to
Jesus, "Your own nation and the chief priests have handed you

over to me" (18:35). It is the chief priests and officers who cry out, "Crucify him, crucify him" (19:6).

This sacrificial interest starts early in the gospel with the story of the call of the beloved disciple by the Jordan River. John the Baptist had first pointed out Jesus with the words, "Behold the Lamb of God who takes away the sins of the world," and later simply "Behold the Lamb of God" (1:29, 36). In the Old Testament sacrifices were necessary for forgiveness of sin. C.K. Barrett[58] has suggested that the Baptist originally took "lamb of God" in a powerful, victorious, apocalyptic sense, but that the gospel transformed and completed its meaning to a sacrificial one connected with Jesus as the new passover sacrifice. The book of Revelation, which has some affinities with the gospel of John, but probably not the same author, has both the sacrificial meaning (5:6, 12; 7:14; 12:11; 13:8) and the victorious triumphant significance (5:8, 12–13; 7:9; 15:3; 22:1, 3).

The Witness at the Cross:
Jesus as the New Passover Sacrifice

First of all, the author carefully establishes a passover atmosphere to prepare for the central witness of the beloved disciple at the foot of the cross (19:35). The central actions of the Jewish passover were the eating of the lamb and the sprinkling of blood on their homes. The eating action is mentioned six times in the ritual directions in Exodus 12. Accordingly, the author notes that the Jews could not enter Pilate's praetorium, "so they might not be defiled, but might eat the passover" (18:28).

Also, the gospel notes that Jesus was condemned and led away on "the day of Preparation of the Passover; it was about the sixth hour" (19:14). This would coincide with the time when the passover lambs were led away to slaughter since they had to be sacrificed before the evening (Ex 12:6). The details of the hyssop used to give Jesus a drink and the basin at the foot of the cross in 19:29 are passover features, for blood was sprinkled on the houses by a hyssop dipped in a basin (Ex 12:22). Finally, the author notes twice that it was the preparation day for the passover in regard to Jesus' body remaining on the cross and being buried (19:31, 42).

In all this, the author's intention is to describe the end of Jesus' life as a parallel and completion to the opening of his ministry where John the Baptist introduced him with the words, "Behold the Lamb of God who takes away the sin of the world" (1:29) and "Behold the lamb of God" (1:36). In both circumstances John the Baptist *saw* Jesus or looked at him when he said these words, just as the chosen disciple actually *saw* the events at the cross (19:35). We shall see later how important this connection between the Baptist and the beloved disciple will be for the gospel audience.

Within this passover setting, the central issue is the description of Jesus' death in terms of a passover lamb sacrifice whose flesh is to be eaten and whose blood will bring life. First of all, in regard to any sacrifice, but especially for the paschal lamb, it was essential that every ritual action had to be done in exact obedience to God. Consequently, the passover ritual was described in detail by God's own words (Ex 12:1), and it is noted that the people did exactly as God ordered: "Then the people of Israel went and did so; as the Lord had commanded Moses and Aaron, so they did" (12:18).

To conform to this obedience motif, the author stresses Jesus' obedience to the Father right until his last breath. The way had already been prepared for this when Jesus stated at his arrest, "Shall I not drink the cup which the Father has given me?" (18:11). As if in application of these words, the author writes of Jesus' last actions as follows: "After this, Jesus, knowing that all was now finished, said (to fulfill the scripture), 'I thirst' " (19:28). The writer has Jesus consciously saying these words in view of the scriptural divine plan of Psalm 69:21 where the innocent servant of God says, "In my thirst they gave me bitter wine to drink."

Special attention is drawn to this *oxos* or bitter wine of Psalm 69:21 which is mentioned three times (19:28–30). Jesus takes this wine as a final act of obedience, for the writer notes that on taking it Jesus said, "It is finished," and then bowed his head and expired (19:30). It is possible that this bowing of his head is also a gesture of obedience like that of the Israelites who bowed their heads in obedience after hearing all of God's words about the passover ritual (Ex 12:27).

Thus Jesus dies in perfect obedience to his Father. Later we will see that this is a model for the obedience of disciples to Jesus' word: Jesus' mother will direct the waiters to do everything that Jesus says (2:5). The "good wine" at the end of the Cana marriage feast will be made possible through obedience to Jesus' word, just as he has obeyed his Father right to the end by accepting the "bitter wine."

The second element in portraying Jesus' death as a passover sacrifice lies in the events that took place on the cross which the writer (and the beloved disciple) understand as the obedient fulfill-ment of God's plan in the scriptures. First of all, he notes that strangely enough the soldiers did not break Jesus' legs as they did with the other two crucified. He sees this as accomplishing the scriptural prescriptions for the *eating* of the paschal lamb: "In one house shall it be eaten; you shall not carry any of the flesh outside the house; and *you shall not break a bone*" (Ex 12:46).

The next part of the scriptural fulfillment refers to the pass-over blood which was an essential sign: "The blood shall be a sign for you, upon the houses where you are; and when I *see* the blood, I will pass over you" (Ex 12:13). The writer emphasizes that he has *seen* this blood flow from the side of Christ: "And at once there came out blood and water. He who saw it has borne witness—his testimony is true, and he knows that he tells the truth—that you also may believe"(19:35). This flow of blood is extremely important because (as J.M. Ford[59] has pointed out) the immediate *flow* of blood was required in Jewish law for a valid sacrifice.

The author recognizes this watery blood as a fulfillment of God's plan in scripture, for he notes, "And another scripture says, 'They shall look on him whom they have pierced' " (19:37); Zech 12:1 according to some Hebrew mss). The context of the Zechariah text may indicate why the author has chosen it. Immedi-ately preceding the above verse we find the words, "I will pour out on the house of David and on the inhabitants of Jerusalem a spirit of grace and petition." Several verses later we find, "On that day there shall be open to the house of David and the inhabitants of Jerusalem a fountain to purify from sin and uncleanness" (Hebrew Massoretic text of Zech 13:1). Blood, of course, was necessary for any purification or forgiveness from sin, of which the text speaks. The sacrificial element is heightened by the use of the word "pierce" or "thrust through" in the Zechariah text. This usually refers to a mortal wound.

Putting it all together, the writer finds a perfect parallel of Jesus to the passover lamb sacrifice. In obedience to the Father, Jesus drank the bitter wine ("blood of the grape" in semitic languages). Therefore, his life/blood became a sacrifice, a prayer-offering to God for forgiveness and life, just as the blood of the passover lambs sprinkled on Jewish homes saved the people from destruction by the plague at the time of the exodus and brought them life (Ex 12:23).

The flow of water may also have been closely connected to Jesus' own prediction as well as to the scriptures. On the last day of the feast of Booths, Jesus had promised, "If anyone thirst, let him come [to me (in most texts)] and let him drink who believes in me. As the scripture says, 'From within him shall flow rivers of living water' " (7:37–38). This is the translation of R.E. Brown in his commentary on John[60] where he details his reasons for understanding the second half ("from within him, etc.") as referring to Jesus rather than to the believer. However, the evangelist in the next verse does note that Jesus was speaking of the Spirit that those who believed in him were to receive, and that this Spirit would only come at Jesus' hour. Consequently, the surprising flow of bloody water from Jesus' side could be understood as confirming Jesus' words that his glorification would bring the gift of the Spirit/water as a result of his bloody sacrifice.

The author, then, has connected Jesus' passover sacrifice of himself with the forgiveness of sins. In this way, it completes John the Baptist's prediction that Jesus would be the lamb of God who takes away the sins of the world (1:29). The water and spirit references would be also important in completing the Baptist's promise that Jesus would be the one who baptizes with the Holy Spirit (1:33). This completion and connection to John the Baptist would be very important for the gospel audience. We have already pointed out that the early church found disciples of the Baptist scattered about the Mediterranean world. These disciples did not acknowledge the effects of Jesus' death nor even know about the Holy Spirit (Acts 18:25; 19:2). Consequently, Paul had to baptize the last group into the saving death of Jesus to experience forgiveness and the gift of the Holy Spirit.

The beloved disciple was the ideal witness to establish a link between believers in the Baptist and "full believers" in Jesus' saving death and its effects. As a close associate with the Baptist, and at the same time Jesus' own favorite disciple, he had a special insight into the meaning of his death. He saw it (at least through the author's eyes) as a complete understanding and fulfillment of the Baptist's proclamation that Jesus was the lamb of God who takes away the sins of the world. Jesus' designation of the beloved disciple as his son/successor at the foot of the cross would give him the important credentials needed to win over former disciples of John the Baptist. To show that John the Baptist's work was incomplete, John's gospel omits any mention that John's baptism brings forgiveness of sins as do Mark 1:4 and Luke 3:3. It is only the sacrificial lamb of God who can take away the sins of the world. (Matthew also omits the "forgiveness of sins" at John's baptism and brings it into the last supper where it is connected with Jesus' sacrificial death and blood—26:28.)

The "priestly connection" of our disciple would also be extremely important for another group addressed by the gospel. These are the "apostolic Christians" who looked to Peter as their founder and inspiration. The gospel's special understanding of the death of Jesus would be very important for this group, since the gospel hints to us that Peter, as representing them, lacked this understanding. This lack seems indicated in the account of the last supper in John.

In this supper account (13:1–38) the central theme is Jesus' approaching death and its significance: "Jesus knew that his hour had come to depart out of this world to the Father" (13:1). With the full knowledge that "the Father had given all things into his hands, and that he had come from God and was going to God,"

Jesus rose from the table and began to wash the feet of his disciples (13:3–5). This action of humble service, from the context, is symbolic of his coming death which will bring forgiveness through its sacrificial nature. When Jesus came to Simon Peter, Peter said, "Lord, do you wash my feet?" Jesus answered, "What I am doing you do not know now, but afterward you will understand." Jesus answered him, "If I do not wash you, you have no part in me" (13:6–8).

From the above, we learn that the footwashing is necessary, that it is something whose meaning will be later seen, and that it is connected with Jesus' death. Peter, however, is reluctant at first to accept it. This links with statements in other gospels about Peter's slowness to accept Jesus' death and its significance. When Jesus first announces that he will suffer and die, Peter objected to it, provoking a strong rebuke from Jesus (Mk 8:31–33; Mt 16:21–23). The disciple at Jesus' bosom represents the very opposite as someone who knows the secret of Jesus' coming death and accepts it. Jesus' command that they are to follow his example and wash the feet of one another brings out that the true disciple must be willing to also sacrifice his or her life for others. Jesus' passover sacrifice for sins must be participatory as well. Consequently, the beloved disciple risks his life in following Jesus even after he has been arrested. At the foot of the cross, along with the women, he risks death by publicly identifying himself with a crucified "criminal." In contrast, Peter follows Jesus only at a distance and openly denies him in the courtyard of the high priest (18:25–27). Only in the gospel "appendix," chapter 21, does Peter appear fully reinstated, with the fulfilled prediction that he finally does die for his master and is worthy to be given the pastoral charge of feeding Jesus' sheep (21:15–19).

We may also note that Paul's letter to the Galatians also hints at Peter's lack of appreciation of the all-embracing effects of the cross. Peter had visited Gentile Christians at Antioch but had refused to eat with them when a group of Jewish Christians appeared on the scene (Gal 2:11–13). Instead, he withdrew and ate only with the latter in order to keep the Jewish food fellowship regulations and customs that forbade eating with Gentiles. Paul insisted that Peter was not true to the gospel and attributed his action to a lack of appreciation of the full efficacy of the cross. He finally states that his own attitude is to be "crucified with Christ" (2:20), and that if justification is to be obtained through conformity with the law, then "Christ has died to no purpose."

By way of summary, we find the following clues about the identity and role of the beloved disciple in regard to his "priestly connection": *The young man came from Judea, probably Jerusalem, and was from a priestly family, or at least strongly associated with one. He had great interest in the Jewish priesthood. He closely followed Jesus in Jerusalem during the last week of his life, and was an actual witness of the unusual events surrounding his death, especially the extraordinary flow of watery blood from his side. Through reflection on the scriptural plan of God, he (or the author) was able to understand Jesus' death as a priestly sacrifice of a new passover lamb for the forgiveness of sins. The gospel makes a close connection link between this insight and the beloved disciple's first teacher, John the Baptist, who had introduced Jesus as the "lamb of God who takes away the sins of the world." With this link, the gospel's author could draw former disciples of the Baptist into communion with himself and others through a deeper appreciation of the meaning of Jesus' death and the gift of the Spirit. It also made it possible for the gospel to provide "apostolic Christians" with additional instruction as to the centrality of Jesus' sacrificial death for complete forgiveness of sins not only for Jewish Christians but for the Gentile world. Jesus as the lamb of God takes away not only the sins of his people, but those of the whole world.*

7

A Young Lad, Five Loaves,
Two Fish, and Jesus' Most Difficult Saying

We have already found several hints that the beloved disciple must have been quite young during the ministry of Jesus. The question whether he would be alive at Jesus' return (21:21–23) indicates this. The image of leaning on the bosom of Jesus at the last supper, and what we have already written about this as applicable to a son/child, also points in this direction. It is interesting that only John's gospel has a boy present the five barley loaves and two fish that will be necessary for Jesus in performing his multiplication of loaves in 6:5–14. Andrew said to Jesus, "There is a lad here who has five barley loaves and two fish" (6:9).

It is not likely that the gospel is trying to say that the beloved disciple was actually this *paidarion* (youth or young man in biblical texts) and an actual witness to the events. However, there are some significant clues that the fourth gospel has this lad *represent* the beloved disciple as furnishing the gospel audience with a special interpretation of the loaves' meaning. The following are these clues.

1. It is "one of the disciples, Andrew, Simon Peter's brother," who presents the young man: "There is a lad here who has five barley loaves and two fish, but what are they among so many?" The description of Andrew is the same as that of John 1:40 where we previously saw that Andrew was the companion of the beloved disciple. In John 1:40 we have, "One of the two who heard John speak, and followed him, was Andrew, Simon Peter's brother."

2. The story fits into the atmosphere of the parallels between Joseph and the beloved disciple. The word *paidarion* is the same word used of the young Joseph in the Greek Septuagint of Genesis 37:30; 42:22. Jesus' question to Philip about where to buy bread (6:5) reminds us of Jacob's question to his sons and his sending them into Egypt to buy wheat (Gen 42:1). Jesus also tests his disciples, just as Joseph tested his brothers (6:6–7; Gen 42:7, 15).

3. The preceding tempting clues are confirmed by the literary structure of the fourth gospel, where the loaves account has a central literary position in direct correlation to the beloved disciple's witness at the cross that Jesus is indeed the new paschal lamb. This literary centrality emerges from the studies of M. Girard,[61] especially the first which we will examine in detail. Girard disagrees with the usual assumption that the first twelve chapters of John contain the principal signs of the gospel. Many bibles even divide the gospel by calling these chapters "the book of signs." Girard writes that it has often been taken for granted that there are seven principal signs in these chapters: (1) the wedding at Cana (2:1–12); (2) the raising of the dying son of the royal official (4:46–54); (3) the sabbath healing of the paralytic; (4) the multiplication of loaves (6:1–15); (5) Jesus' walking on water (6:16–22); (6) the sabbath healing of the blind man (9:1–41); (7) the restoration of Lazarus to life (11:1–54).

However, Girard has brought forth important considerations to show that the evangelist did not intend the above arrangement. We will summarize his arguments because they will be a helpful basis to illustrate the centrality of the loaves section and the important part played by the beloved disciple in its explanation. First of all, Girard accepts R.E. Brown's definition[62] of a sign as a prodigious deed with strong symbolism illustrating Jesus' salvific message. In view of this definition, "sign" four, Jesus' walking on water, simply does not fit. Instead it appears as a part of the total message of the loaves discourse, perhaps bringing out a passover context. Secondly, the actual use of the word "sign" is another indication. The walking on the water contains no mention of this word in contrast to all the others: 2:11; 4:54; 6:2 (in reference to the previous healing at Bethesda); 9:16 and 12:18 referring to the raising of Lazarus.

This however leaves us with only six signs. What is the seventh sign, if there is one? The evangelist does appear to be counting them: he calls Cana the first (2:11), and names the second as the raising of the official's son (4:54). It would appear strange for him to have only six signs like the incomplete six water jars at Cana! In looking for a seventh sign, there is really no strong reason to conclude the signs with the so-called end of the signs book in 12:37–50 where the author writes, "Though he had done so many signs before them, yet they did not believe in him" (12:37). This may only mean that the previous *six* signs are incomplete and insufficient. This hypothesis is strengthened by the author's conclusion (if chapter 21 is an appendix) after Jesus' death that "these (signs) have been written that you may believe that Jesus is the Christ, the Son of God"(20:31).

For Girard, the real seventh sign is Jesus' death and the extraordinary issue of blood and water from Jesus' side. The beloved disciple who saw it considers it so unusual that he stressed that he was an eyewitness relating it so that others may believe as well (19:35). As a result, the first six signs are meant to be incomplete and point to the seventh at Jesus' hour when he will be lifted up and draw the world to himself (12:32–33). The specific word "sign" is not used during the seventh, perhaps because the author wished to save it for his final conclusion in 20:31 (quoted above).

However, I would like to suggest that the passover connections we brought out in the last chapter are so strong that the audience would surely realize that meaning of the passover ritual came to a climax with the "sign of the blood" of the passover lamb: "The blood shall be a sign for you, upon the houses where you are; and when I see the blood, I will pass over you, and no plague shall fall upon you to destroy you" (Ex 12:13). The beloved disciple actually *saw* the sign of the blood as he stood beneath the cross (19:35).

With this seventh sign, Girard has discovered the following chiastic structure of the seven signs:

(1) The wedding feast at Cana (2:1–12)
  (2) The raising of the dying son of the official (4:46–54)
    (3) The sabbath healing at Bethesda (5:1–16)
      (4) The loaves' multiplication and the bread
        of life (6:1–71)
    (5) The sabbath healing of the blind man (9:1–41)
  (6) The raising of Lazarus (11:1–41)
(7) The hour of Jesus and the issue of blood
  and water (19:25–38)

We immediately notice the general correspondence above: (3) and (5) are both sabbath healings; (2) and (6) contain the same death to life themes because of Jesus' word; (1) and (7) complement one another as beginning and end, with Jesus' mother present in both, witnessing Jesus' obedience to his Father on the cross, culminating with the drink of bitter wine according to the scriptures. In parallel, at Cana, Mary asks for obedience to Jesus' word which culminates in the chief steward's taking the "cup" of good wine.

It is quite evident that the sign of the loaves stands in the center of the literary ladder, with all the others pointing to it and completing its meaning, especially the seventh sign on the cross. In confirmation of this central literary position, the most severe crisis of the gospel occurs at this point: many disciples of Jesus part from him because of his difficult saying about eating his flesh and drinking his blood (6:60–61). Jesus points to sign seven as the key to understanding: What if you were to *see* the Son of Man ascending where he was before; it is the spirit that gives life, the flesh is of no use" (6:62–63). Finally, Peter's confession comes at this point as an affirmation of belief, despite Jesus' difficult saying (6:68–69).

There are also some literary interconnections between the sign of the loaves and the seventh sign on the cross that are unique: Jesus' "blood" found four times in 6:53–56 is only mentioned again in the flow of blood from his side in 19:34. Jesus' mother is only found in the first sign at Cana, at the seventh sign by the cross, and in the fourth sign of the loaves regarding Jesus' origins when the Jews ask, "Is this not Jesus, the son of Joseph, whose father and mother we know?" (6:42 according to many Greek texts). It should also be mentioned that in the sign of the loaves we have the presence of Peter along with Judas, who represents those who do not believe (6:68–71). This disbelief and betrayal will emerge again at the last supper where the washing of feet (as previously shown) was a prophetic action of Jesus' death. Only at the last supper do we also have Peter, Judas, and of course the beloved disciple.

Therefore, we would expect that the seventh sign, the beloved disciple's essential witness of the death of Jesus and the watery blood from his side, would be the key to understanding the fourth sign of the loaves. This is hinted at in Jesus' statement that only when they *see* the Son of Man ascending will they know that his words are spirit and life (6:62–63). We have already noted that the issue of water from Jesus' side was a sign that his death was the source of the Spirit, and therefore he must have ascended into heaven.

The most important part of the sign of the loaves is the difficult saying about eating Jesus' flesh and drinking his blood which caused so many disciples to leave him (6:51–54, 60–66). This can only find its meaning on the cross. In the last chapter, we pointed out that the beloved disciple saw and witnessed the issue of watery blood from Jesus' side, and that this made him conclude that Jesus was indeed the new sacrificial passover lamb who takes away the sins of the world. But how to participate in this event? The Jewish passover regulations, given by God himself, were a key. Central to the ritual was the *eating* of the paschal lamb and the blood of the lamb sprinkled on their homes that granted them divine protection.

In regard to the first element, the *eating,* God had directed, "In one house shall it be eaten; you shall not carry any of the flesh outside the house; and you shall not break a bone" (Ex 12:46). The beloved disciple bore witness that this scripture was fulfilled in the manner of Jesus' death (19:35–37). It should be noted that the Hebrew text specifically mentions the *bashar* or flesh of the lamb in Exodus 12:8, where it is said, "You shall eat the flesh that night." This would correspond to Jesus' words in the loaves sign, 6:51, where he speaks of eating his flesh. The Greek Old Testament has the words *ta krea* for the flesh, but the *sarx* root used by Jesus in John 6:51–56 is also used of the flesh of sacrifice in Leviticus 4:11 and in 17:11 where it is written that the "life of the flesh is in the blood."

The second element in the passover nature of Jesus' death concerns the blood of the lamb: "The blood shall be a sign for you, upon the houses where you are; and when I *see* the blood, I will pass over you" (Ex 12:13). The beloved disciple *saw* this sacrificial blood issue from the side of Christ: "And at once there came out blood and water. He who saw it has borne witness—and his testimony is true, and he knows that he tells the truth—that you also may believe" (19:35). In connection with this blood we noted in the last chapter the emphasis on scripture fulfillment. Here we will draw attention to the connection to Jesus' saying about "drinking his blood" in the loaves sign where this is repeated three times for emphasis in 6:53–56. This is especially connected to the text in Zechariah quoted by the evangelist: "They shall look on him whom they have pierced" (19:37; Zech 12:10). We also stated that a few verses later the prophet writes, "On that day there shall be open to the house of David and the inhabitants of Jerusalem a fountain to purify from sin and uncleanness" (MT Zech 13:1). The text speaks of purification from sin, for which a flow of blood was required. The use of the word "fountain" is important since this is a common word for a drinking source, and thus would correspond to Jesus' words about drinking his blood (6:51–56).

Consequently, the writer, on the beloved disciple's testimony, relates Jesus' words on eating his flesh and drinking his blood to the passover lamb ritual as embodied by Jesus on the cross. Jesus drank the bitter wine, "blood of the grape," on the cross in obedience to the scriptures in accord with his words, "Shall I not drink the cup which the Father has given me? (18:11). Therefore his blood/life became a sacrifice or a prayer-offering to God for forgiveness and life, just as the blood of the passover lambs sprinkled on Jewish homes saved Israel from destruction at the time of the Exodus (12:23) and brought them life. In the Old Testament God had said, "The blood shall be a sign for you" (12:13). Likewise, on the cross, the ultimate sign is the sacrificial blood flowing from Christ in such an unusual symbolic manner.

However, how will the believer be able to ritually eat the new passover and "drink" the fruits of the blood of sacrifice? This will be shown in the first sign at Cana, which will be studied in the next chapter. The literary structure hints that the first and seventh signs are interconnected and together explain the fourth sign, especially Jesus' most difficult saying about consuming his flesh and blood.

In conclusion, we add the following additional clues: *The interconnections between the loaves sign and the seventh sign on the cross strengthen the suggestion that the beloved disciple is represented by the young lad with the five loaves and two fish. He is the one who presents the loaves and explains their meaning through the seventh sign on the cross: Jesus the new paschal lamb whose flesh and blood are to be consumed. Peter adds his external authority at the end through his faith confession (6:69), but it is the beloved disciple who provides the inner understanding of the loaves, especially Jesus' difficult sayings about eating his flesh and drinking his blood. This gave him a special mission to explain this meaning both to former disciples of the Baptist and to Jewish Christians, including "apostolic Christians" who based their teachings on Peter's authority.*

8

The Mother of Jesus and
of the Beloved Disciple[63]

Jesus' mother is a central figure in the fourth gospel. She is also very closely linked with the beloved disciple in view of Jesus' last words directing her to take his favorite disciple as her own son, and reciprocally for him to take her as his own mother:

> Standing by the cross of Jesus were his mother, and his mother's sister, Mary of Clopas, and Mary Magdalene. When Jesus saw his mother, and the disciple whom he loved standing near, he said to his mother, "Woman, behold your son!" Then he said to the disciple, "Behold your mother!" And from that hour the disciple took her to his own home (19:25–28).

This essential place of Mary is strengthened by the literary structure of the seven signs: Jesus' mother is present at the first sign at Cana (2:1–11) and at the seventh sign at the cross (19:25–37). She is also named in the central loaves sign (6:42, most mss). Any serious investigation of the beloved disciple would necessitate an understanding of Mary's role in the gospel. The best place to start is at the unusual scene at the foot of the cross in the seventh sign.

The Mother of Jesus and the Beloved Disciple
in the Seventh Sign (19:25–37)

First of all, we note that Mary's presence is not incidental, but central in the first and last signs. Her name and presence open and close the first sign at Cana, as well as the last sign at the cross.

In the first sign, the word "mother" is used four times, and "woman" once (2:1–11); in the seventh sign, "mother" is likewise found four times and "woman" once (19:25, 26, 27). Thus the writer intends a close connection between the two episodes.

The seventh sign begins with the simple statement that Jesus' mother stood by the cross along with other women—and the close disciple in the next verse. At face value she would be a most important witness, along with him, of these central events. The question of historicity (since she is not at the cross in the other gospels) need not detain us: the evangelist uses the words "see" and know in deeper senses. Even the blind can "see" if they are open to Jesus' words (9:39). By the time John's gospel was written, Jesus' mother had probably been dead for many years, yet the author wrote as if the events described were of present significance to his audience: "he tells the truth that you also may believe" (19:35). Perhaps the evangelist understood the scene at the cross not as an event in the past but as a timeless drama. The risen Jesus always bears the marks of the cross and the spear (20:20, 24). At any rate, we are taking the gospel "as is" for our primary source.

During the seventh sign, the beloved disciple makes his most important statement in the gospel as a solemn eyewitness testimony when he sees the watery blood issue from Jesus' side after the lance thrust: "He who saw it has borne witness—his testimony is true, and he knows that he tells the truth—that you also may believe" (19:35). In previous chapters, we have studied the significance of this statement and the accompanying events: they point to Jesus as the true passover sacrificial lamb whose flesh is to be consumed and whose sprinkled blood brings salvation. Such an essential matter requires an unmistakable stamp of credibility. We have already shown that Jesus' last will established the blessed disciple as his successor and son by having his own mother continue the relationship by adopting the blessed disciple as her own son.

In addition, Jesus' mother functions as a joint witness along with the beloved disciple of these key events in Jesus' life and their meaning. Together they witness the seventh sign which culminates in the unusual prodigy of watery blood flowing from Jesus' side. First of all, Mary acts as a mother in testifying to the utter reality of Jesus' death. The popular perception of the indelible memory of a mother for her child is found in Isaiah 49:15, where God says, "Can a woman forget her sucking child, that she should have no compassion on the son of her womb?" This would especially be true of a child's death. Mary would be a mother to the community of the beloved disciple as a carrier of tradition, as one who remembers, which is a supreme function of a mother. Her association with Jesus in any explanation of his person or mission would be a continual reminder of his death and its meaning.

As we have noted, the seventh and first signs complete the meaning of the fourth sign of the loaves and answer questions there about it. The question of Jesus' humanity and death would be very important for understanding the central sign of the loaves. The joint witness of Jesus' mother and the disciple would be necessary to answer questions about the flesh-and-blood reality of Jesus in the sign of the loaves and to explain that it is a bread which the Son of Man gives (6:27, 53, 62). In addition, the mother's witness to Jesus' humanity in his birth would be essential. This is alluded to in 6:42 where it is mentioned that Jesus' father and mother are known.

Beyond the reality of Jesus' death, the gospel also has a very special interest in *how* Jesus died. Mary is presented as an essential witness of this. The first important matter is that Jesus died on the cross in perfect obedience to his Father. In the gospel presentation of this, Jesus' obedience to God's plan as found in the scriptures is a dominant theme (19:24, 28, 30). As already noted, special focus is placed on Psalm 69:21, "In my thirst they gave me bitter wine to drink." The evangelist pictures Jesus as very consciously saying, "I thirst," and taking the wine in order to fulfill God's scriptural plan. We also noted the stress on this *oxos* or bitter wine of Psalm 69:21 which is repeated three times in 19:28–30. It is this wine that Jesus takes in obedience.

Later we will see in the first sign that Mary will direct the "waiters" to do everything that Jesus says (2:5). The "good wine" will be made possible through obedience to Jesus' word, just as he has been obedient to the Father on the cross by accepting the "bitter wine." The very last words of Jesus after taking the wine are, "It is finished (or completed)" (19:30). He has been obedient right to his last action of drinking the "final cup" of bitter wine. Thus he has completed his own life as well as God's plan in the scriptures. In this way, the words of Jesus at his arrest are literally fulfilled: "Shall I not drink the cup which the Father has given me?" (18:11).

In addition to this obedience motif, Jesus' mother is also a key witness of an unusual death that brings out a divine element within Jesus: he appears supremely in control on the cross. He knows exactly when he is going to die (19:28); then he says that it is all finished (19:30); and finally he seems deliberately to bow his head and expire. This was anticipated in 10:18 where Jesus said that no one takes away his life from him; he dies by his own choice. He has the power to give (or lay down) his life and to take it up again in accord with the Father's command. This sign points to something supra-human in Jesus' death. It is surely a real death, yet no human being has the power to determine when life will come and when it will go.

In the prologue the author described how the Word came into the world to be born in the flesh by his own choice; now he dies in the same way. All of this points to a divine element in Jesus, and his mother is a witness of this. With our interconnection to the loaves sign, this would provide an answer to the question in the sign of the loaves, "How does he now say, 'I have come down from heaven'?" (6:42). It is significant that, immediately after this, in the next verse, Jesus' mother is mentioned. This voluntary picture of Jesus' death would also be essential to show that he is the real priest who offers himself, the paschal lamb, to the Father. The Jewish priests and Pilate are only indirect instruments that God has allowed to function in this way.

Finally, in regard to *how Jesus died,* the role of his mother reaches its highest peak in regard to the motivation for his death. While this motivation lies in obedience to the Father, it is not a mechanical conformity but an obedience prompted by love and concern for his disciples. The will of the Father is to save his beloved human family. Thus Jesus says, "It is the will of him who sent me that I should lose nothing of what he has given me; rather I should raise it up on the last day" (6:39; also, 17:12). Before the final supper, the evangelist remarks that Jesus loved his disciples "to the end" (13:1).

This "to the end" may simply mean to the fullest extent, but it is hard to exclude the end or completion on the cross when Jesus said it was finished (19:30). This motivation is confirmed in the sixth sign, the raising of Lazarus. When Jesus resolved to go to Lazarus in Judea, his disciples were alarmed because they knew the master's life was in danger (11:8). However, Jesus decided to go, knowing this would mean his own death. Thus the writer brings out symbolically (the raising of Lazarus being the sign of the raising of Christians) that Jesus died out of love in order to make others live. For this reason, the author stresses that Jesus loved Lazarus, Martha, and Mary (11:5). Mary at the foot of the cross is also a witness of this motivating love along with the beloved disciple.

To sum up: Jesus' mother at the foot of the cross is a person who can guarantee the authenticity of the beloved disciple's teaching on the reality and meaning of Jesus' death. She can do this because of Jesus' last wishes establishing the beloved disciple as her son. This confirms the relationship of the beloved disciple as Jesus' own son and successor. Mary also serves as a witness along with the beloved disciple of the reality of Jesus' humanity as well as his divinity. She confirms the meaning of Jesus' death as the new passover lamb, thus showing how Jesus can ask in the loaves sign that his flesh be eaten and his blood consumed (6:52–55). As to how the believer will actually be able to do this is explained in the first sign at Cana which will now be discussed.

Jesus' Mother in the First Sign,
Cana of Galilee (2:1–12)

Because of the chiastic arrangement of the seven signs, we would expect the first, fourth, and seventh signs to have a close relationship. The first is included in the last, and the last completes the first; both illustrate the loaves sign. On the surface, there are common elements to all three, especially the first and last: Jesus' mother, the "hour" on the cross (2:4), the thirst or lack of wine, the obedience motif, the wine/blood/water. There is no direct mention of the beloved disciple in this story. However, the event immediately follows the call of the beloved disciple and Jesus' first disciples who presumably accompany him to Cana. At any rate, the strong connections between this event and the beloved disciple's witness at the seventh sign point to his great influence, if not actual presence, in regard to the Cana sign.

The Cana story opens with the mother of Jesus present at a wedding, and with Jesus and his disciples also invited. Of course, a wedding feast is a well-known symbol of the messianic days (Is 54:4–8; 62:4–5). The wedding and the banquet are symbols used elsewhere by Jesus (Mt 8:11; 9:15; 22:1–14). Abundant wine is the main ingredient of such festivities. To run short on such an occasion would be a long-remembered public embarrassment for any married couple. On her own initiative, or at the behest of the guests or family, Mary brings up the matter to Jesus and says, "They have no wine." Jesus responds (literally), "What is it to me and to you, woman? My hour has not yet come" (2:4).

Jesus' reply to Mary appears to have a negative nuance. However, C.H. Giblin[64] has pointed out through Johannine parallels that the words do not necessarily mean a refusal to act. They imply that, if Jesus acts, it will be in accord with *his own* conscious purpose and design, not that of others. Therefore, at Cana he will not act according to the expectations of Mary or the people, but in line with his *hour*. This hour will be his glorification on the cross which will expose his true relationship with the Father and with his people. What Jesus wants to accomplish at Cana will be shown only through the seventh and last sign at the cross. This means that the initial type of miracle requested by Mary/the people is not in Jesus' design.

This rejection of a "wonder work" seems to parallel the interconnected fourth sign of the loaves. There the people misunderstand Jesus' miracle and understand it in the sense that Jesus will be another Moses, a wonder-worker bringing miraculous bread like that provided by Moses in the desert. Jesus refuses to accept this definition of his role. He withdrew from the crowd, fearing they would try to make him king (6:14). In the situation of the Johannine community, this might refer to Jewish Christians whose views of Jesus were limited to that of a messiah and sign-worker.[65] If the purpose of Jesus' mother in the story reflects this, then Jesus refuses to act out of this motive, but only in view of the approaching hour on the cross and the meaning of his death in the seventh sign.

Following the statement about Jesus' hour, his mother tells the waiters, "Do whatever he tells you" (2:5). Jesus' mother now acts toward the waiters (and the community) in accord with the maternal remembering role emphasized in the seventh sign. The emphasis is on perfect obedience to Jesus' word. This is noted three times: by Mary's word, by the waiters' filling the jars as Jesus directed, and by their obedience to his command to bring the jars to the chief steward. We note the parallel to the seventh sign, where Jesus obeys the scriptures and the divine plan by taking the imperfect bitter wine as the cup of suffering prepared by the Father (19:28–30). Thus Mary directs the community to obey Jesus' words, just as he has obeyed his Father's.

What words of Jesus are they to obey? In view of the interconnection to the central sign of the loaves, the answer should be there. The whole crisis in this sign is the triple statement of Jesus that his flesh must be eaten and his blood drunk (6:51–56). How is this to be done? The seventh sign has shown that Jesus is indeed the new paschal lamb sacrifice. The first sign seems to give the key as to how the believer can "consume" or be part of that sacrifice. The difficult command of Jesus can be obeyed by the believer in the same way as Jesus obeyed on the cross. There he accepted the "cup" of imperfect bitter wine or "blood of the grape" in obedience to the Father. At Cana, we note that the taking of the "cup" of good wine to the chief steward was the final action of a chain of obedience to Jesus' words. This may hint at the ritual way the believer can participate: by taking, in obedience to Jesus' word, the cup of the "blood of the grape" just as Jesus did. This emphasis on the cup has its parallel in Luke's account of the last supper where the cup is mentioned three times in the longer Greek form of 22:17–20. It is also mentioned first by Paul in 1 Corinthians 10:16 and emphasized in 1 Corinthians 10:21.

Jesus' Mother and the Beloved Disciple: An Intimate Relationship

We have seen the association of these two as joint witnesses at the most important moments in Jesus' life, and in sharing an understanding of their meaning. Already this amounts to a deep communion between them. In addition, it was essential that the beloved disciple establish his credibility as Jesus' favorite disciple, son and successor for the gospel audience. The best way to show this was in recalling Jesus' last words directing that his own mother continue the relationship by adopting the beloved disciple as her own son.

However, there is another consideration that may lead us to posit an intimate relationship between the two. If, as suggested in previous chapters, Jesus adopted the beloved disciple as a young man, this may have been due to the fact that he had lost his mother or parents at an early age. Perhaps John the Baptist first took him in as a protégé for this reason. Here again there is a resemblance between the beloved disciple and his prototype Joseph who while still a youngster lost his mother during the birth of his younger brother Benjamin (35:16–21). If this is so, the beloved disciple's relationship to Jesus would have been his closest male bond, and, quite naturally, that to Jesus' mother his closest female tie. This appears confirmed at the foot of the cross. The adoption pictured there does not seem to be merely formal. At the end, it is written that the "disciple took her to his own [home]" (19:27). This seems to imply that he lived with her in the close ties of a son, replacing Jesus her beloved first-born in the family.

We may briefly summarize the clues from this chapter: *There were intimate ties between Mary and the beloved disciple. He was her adopted son after Jesus' death and replaced his presence in the family as almost a twin of her first-born son. Since Mary was probably a widow by this time,*[66] *this relationship would be all the more meaningful. There was also a deep communion between the two because they alone shared a unique insight on the meaning of Jesus' life and especially his death. This resulted from their joint witness at his death and the unusual circumstances surrounding it. The association of Jesus' mother and the beloved disciple gave a special credibility and authority to the beloved disciple as a chosen witness, favorite son and successor of Jesus.*

9
Disciple of Love
and Model of Relationships

In this chapter we will focus more on the role that the beloved disciple plays in the gospel than on his identity. The role as a model of relationships must be studied within the total movement of the gospel. This is designed to present *who Jesus is* in terms of the loving self-disclosure of God to the *cosmos,* especially humankind. This starts with God's own mirror of himself in the eternal creative *Logos* described in the opening gospel words:

> In the beginning was the Word, and the Word was with God, and the Word was God. He was in the beginning with God. All things were made through him, and without him was not anything made that was made. In him was life, and the life was the light of human beings.

However, it reaches its climactic point in the Logos becoming human flesh and dwelling among human beings in order to make them children of God and temples of the divinity like Jesus:

> He came to his own home, and his own people received him not. But to all who received him, who believed in his name, he gave power to become children of God. . . . And the Word became flesh and dwelt among us, full of grace and truth; we have beheld his glory, glory as of the only Son from the Father (1:12–14).

Jesus in turn is the full revelation of the divine Logos to the world. He makes it possible for God to be seen, known and loved since he reveals the inner secrets of God to human beings. So the author writes, "No one has ever seen God; the only Son, who is in the bosom of the Father, he has made him known" (1:18). Thus we have the revelatory sequence God → Logos/Son/Jesus → Disciples → World.

In this sequence, God's relationship to his Son Jesus becomes the pattern for Jesus' relationship to his disciples. Here is where the beloved disciple has a key role. Just as Jesus the Son rests in the Father's bosom, knows his secrets and reveals them to others, so also does the beloved disciple. He is at the bosom of Jesus at the last supper (13:23). There he learns Jesus' great secret of his future betrayal and reveals this to Peter (13:23–26). This basic pattern emerges in other places also. The role of the beloved disciple is to be the visible embodiment of Jesus' own relationship to his disciples. We will try to point this out in three representative areas: (1) in regard to the Holy Spirit or Paraclete; (2) as a model for those whom Jesus loves, especially in a family setting; (3) in the beloved disciple's counterpart, Mary Magdalene.

The Beloved Disciple, Manifestation of the Holy Spirit/Paraclete

Jesus' last words and final testament to his disciples are found in his final discourse, chapters 14–17. This was a familiar literary pattern to the audience. E. Käsemann notes, "In the composition of chapter 17, the Evangelist undoubtedly used a literary device which is common in world literature and employed by Judaism as well as by New Testament writers. It is the device of the farewell speech of a dying man."[67] A close reading of these chapters reveals a striking parallel between the function of the Holy Spirit and the beloved disciple. They are so closely related that the beloved disciple appears as a special manifestation of this Spirit.

Alan Culpepper has developed this theme of the beloved disciple as manifestation of the Spirit. He writes as follows,

The similarity between Jesus' words regarding what the Paraclete would do after his death and the allusions to what the Beloved Disciple did after Jesus' death are suggestive. The Paraclete was to remain with the disciples (14:17), teach them everything (14:26), remind the disciples of all that Jesus had said (14:26), declare what he has heard (16:13), and glorify Jesus because he will "receive from me [Jesus] and declare to you" (16:14). From all indications this is exactly what the Beloved Disciple has done. He has come from the bosom of Jesus and has made him known to those who now affirm his testimony. He has taught, reminded, and borne a true witness. The words of Jesus in the gospel are the words that he has received from the Lord and written or caused to be written. The Beloved Disciple is not the Paraclete, of course, but he has embodied the Paraclete for others. In him, belief, love, and faithful witness are joined. He abides in Jesus' love, and the Paraclete works through him.[68]

One Whom Jesus Loves—
Model for All Those Whom Jesus Loves

The one, or disciple, whom Jesus loved is the principal designation of the disciple in this gospel (13:23; 19:26; 20:2; 21:7, 20). This love is parallel to and modeled on the love of the Father for Jesus. This is shown in statements like, "The Father loves the Son, and has given all things into his hand" (cf. also 5:20; 10:17; 15:9). The last text especially brings out that this love is a model for Jesus' love of the disciples: "As the Father has loved me, so also I love you; abide in my love." Consequently, the title "the one, or disciple whom Jesus loved" represents this special love of Jesus which is embodied in the concrete figure of the beloved disciple.

It is not surprising that the same designation will be used for other disciples as well. A prominent example is the "family relationship" of Jesus with Lazarus, Martha and Mary. When Lazarus became seriously ill, the two sisters sent to him, saying, "Lord, he whom you love is ill" (11:3). We note here the phrase, "the one whom you love," the same designation as that of the beloved disciple. Also the text adds, "Now Jesus loved Martha and her sister and Lazarus," to make the family picture of love complete (11:5). Jesus' love for Lazarus continues even after Lazarus' death, for the Jews remark at the tomb, upon seeing Jesus weeping, "See how he loved him!" (11:36).

In the story the quality of this love receives special attention. Jesus responds to the message about Lazarus' illness by saying, "Let us go into Judea again." His disciples know well that Jesus risks death by going there to help Lazarus. They answer, "Rabbi, the Jews were but now seeking to stone you and are you going there again?" (11:8). The whole story brings out a central gospel message—that Jesus is willing to lay down his own life for love of others so they may have eternal life. In this case it is for Lazarus and his sisters. Thus Jesus fulfills his own words, "Greater love has no one than this, that a person lay down life itself for friends" (15:12).

Martha responds to Jesus' love by a great act of faith in Jesus despite the human impossibility of his promise to raise Lazarus. Jesus says to her, "Do you believe this?" She answers, "Yes, Lord, I believe that you are the Christ, the Son of God, he who is coming into the world" (11:27). Mary's response appears to be an inner and deeply personal one. It will be illustrated in the Bethany anointing. Here, as throughout the gospel, we are not interested in trying to understand what originally may have happened, or to uncover various layers of editorship. We presume that the gospel was written in its final form in narrative drama with a special message to the audience that could be understood by them.

> Six days before the Passover, Jesus came to Bethany, where Lazarus was whom Jesus had raised from the dead. There they made him a supper. Martha served, and Lazarus was one of those at table with him. Mary took a pound of costly ointment of pure nard and anointed the feet of Jesus and wiped his feet with her hair; and the house was filled with the fragrance of the ointment (12:1–3).

The atmosphere of the story is a family reception for Jesus before the passover and his death. Martha fulfills her family role in table service as in Luke's story (10:38–42). Mary, however, takes on a hostess role as she welcomes the important guest by the customary washing of feet. However, it is described as an action of extraordinary devotion and love. This is shown in two ways: first by the extremely expensive ointment, a symbol of her own self-giving; second, by letting down her hair and wiping his feet. Anne Winsor[69] has illustrated this action as a special symbol of love in the light of feminist exegesis of the text.

The phrase, "the house was filled with the odor of the ointment" (12:3), symbolizes the far-reaching effects of this family reception of Jesus. It appears to echo the words of the prologue, "To all who received him, who believed in his name, he gave power to become children of God" (1:12). This reception of Jesus prepares the way for his own washing of the disciples' feet in response to Mary's action. Jesus washes his disciples' feet as a final act of reception and hospitality[70] in order to bring the disciples into the heavenly home to which he is returning. The story begins with the words, "Jesus knew that the hour had come to depart out of this world to the Father" (13:1).

Mary Magdalene:
Counterpart of the Beloved Disciple

During the supreme moments of Jesus' last hour, Mary Magdalene stands side by side with the beloved disciple and Jesus' mother (19:25). As the beloved disciple becomes the inner successor of Jesus for the Johannine community, so Mary Magdalene becomes the indispensable link to apostolic Christians under Peter's leadership. This is because she is the apostle of apostles, the one who first sees the risen Jesus, receives a commission from him, and then notifies the others to assemble for Jesus' ascension and the gift of the Holy Spirit. All of this results from her special relationship to Jesus, which is a counterpart to that of the beloved disciple. The author describes this, basing his views on the witness

of the beloved disciple both at the cross and in the resurrection
story. These stories point to a very special relationship to Jesus,
like that of the beloved disciple.

This unique relationship is portrayed by the detailed narra-
tion of the encounter of Mary Magdalene with the risen Jesus.
Mary was so anxious to visit Jesus' tomb that she arose while it
was still dark after a sleepless night. While the other gospels
describe other women coming with her, John's gospel singles her
out for her unusual devotion and special relationship to Jesus,
which would be a model for the true believer. Mary was com-
pletely shocked to find that the circular stone at the burial cave
entrance had been rolled aside. Fearing that a grave robbery
might have taken place, she ran as fast as she could to notify Peter
and "the other disciple Jesus loved." She said to them, "They
have taken the Lord out of the tomb, and we do not know where
they have laid him" (20:1–2). Both men ran to the tomb to verify
her statement and found indeed that the body was missing, but no
signs of it being stolen: the shroud was lying on the ground, and
the face covering (*soudarion)* was rolled in a place by itself. No
tomb robbers would have taken the time to unwrap the body and
leave everything so neatly.

Shocked and dazed by not finding the body of Jesus, Mary
stood outside the tomb and wept. She bent down to look again
inside the tomb and saw two angels in bright robes sitting at the
head and foot of the place where Jesus' body had been. They said,
"Woman, why are you weeping?" (20:13). Mary replied, "Because they have taken away my Lord, and I do not know where
they have laid him." Turning around, she saw a man standing
there whom she took to be the gardener, not recognizing him as
Jesus. He said to her, "Woman, why are you weeping?" She said
to him, "Sir, if you have carried him away, tell me where you have
laid him, and I will take him away." By this threefold repetition of
Mary's words, the gospel writer draws attention to Mary's ardent
longing to see the Jesus she loved so much.

> Jesus said to her, "Mary." She turned and said to him in He-
> brew "Rabboni!" (which means Teacher). Jesus said to her,

"Do not hold me, for I have not yet ascended to the Father. But go to my brethren and say to them, 'I am ascending to my Father and your Father, to my God and your God' " (20:16–17).

Mary recognizes Jesus only when he calls her by name. R.E. Brown[71] notes that this is a special privilege in John's gospel. As good shepherd, Jesus calls only his own sheep by name (10:3). They alone are his very own (10:14). The evangelist highlights the encounter of Mary and Jesus by noting the exact word that Mary would use in Aramaic, *Rabboni*, meaning "Master" or "Teacher." Mary Magdalene is privileged to be the first one to see the risen Jesus because of her great love and strong desire to see him. Then Jesus gives her the unique privilege of being the first one to announce to others that he has risen from the dead.

In view of the Old Testament background, the story of the encounter between Mary and Jesus resembles that between a bridegroom and spouse. During the Passover season, the love poems of the Song of Songs were read in the synagogue. As people listened to the songs that the bride and bridegroom recited to one another, they thought of God's own love for his people Israel. The following passage seems especially significant:

> Upon my bed by night I sought him whom my soul loves; I sought him, but found him not. . . . I will rise now and go about the city, in the streets and in the squares; I will seek him whom my soul loves. I sought him, but found him not. The watchmen found me as they went about in the city. "Have you seen him whom my soul loves?" Scarcely had I passed them when I found him whom my soul loves. I held him, and would not let him go (Song 3:1–4).

The correspondence with the encounter between Mary and Jesus is striking. M. Cambe[72] has pointed out the following details: the night atmosphere (John 20:21); the triple searching of the bride for her lover; the question addressed to the watchmen (the same word as "gardener" in Hebrew); finally, taking hold of him and not willing to let him go. In this manner, John's gospel may be illustrating the inner meaning of the relationship between Mary and Jesus. It is similar to the covenant union of bridegroom and beloved in the Song of Songs.

This espousal theme is also found elsewhere in the scriptures where God's union with his people is described in nuptial terms. For example, God spoke through Hosea his prophet as follows:

> I will betroth you to me for ever; I will betroth you to me in faithfulness and in justice, in steadfast love, and in mercy. I will betroth you to me in faithfulness; and you shall know the Lord (2:19–20).

In the New Testament, the apostle Paul used similar terminology in writing to the Corinthians about their relationship to Christ: "I feel a divine jealousy for you, for I betrothed you to Christ to present you as a pure bride to her one husband" (2 Cor 11:2). The book of Revelation pictured the final stage of the kingdom of God as "the marriage of the Lamb."

Mary Magdalene, Apostle of Apostles and Inner Successor with the Beloved Disciple

By such a careful picture of Mary's close union with Jesus and her role as model of believers, the author presents us with a remarkable parallel to the intimate relationship between the beloved disciple and Jesus. Both are inner successors, each in a unique way, to Jesus. As with the beloved disciple, her role is best seen in comparison and in contrast with others, especially Peter. Mary alone risks the danger of going by herself to the tomb while it was still dark (20:1), for all followers of the crucified one must have been suspect. She is the first to notice that it is empty and runs as fast as she can to tell Peter and "the other disciple whom Jesus loved" (20:2). The two disciples verify the empty tomb, and the beloved disciple believes on seeing the face cloth or *soudarion* (more on this "sign" in the next chapter). Peter, however, does not yet believe. Both disciples then return to the safety of home: "Then the disciples went back to their homes" (20:10).

Mary, however, in her overwhelming grief and desire to find the Lord, remains by the tomb, despite the risk. First, angels in a vision say to her, "Woman, why are you weeping?" (20:13). Then the risen Lord, unrecognized by her, asks the same question. Finally her persistence and faith lead to Jesus manifesting himself to her. Jesus said to her,

> Do not hold me, for I have not yet ascended to the Father; but go to my brethren and say to them, I am ascending to my Father and your Father, to my God and your God (20:17).

The author stresses this mission of Mary to the others by noting its accomplishment: "Mary Magdalene went and said to the disciples, 'I have seen the Lord'; and she told them that he had said these things to her" (20:18).

Consequently, Mary Magdalene's testimony makes possible the first gathering of the twelve (and future Christianity). In this way she has an essential inner formative role as apostle to the apostles. In contrast, only in the "appendix," chapter 21, is Peter confirmed in the more external and shepherd role when Jesus says to him, "Feed my sheep" (21:15–17).

The term "apostle" as used of Mary is not in the sense of one of the twelve. It has the special meaning of one who has seen the risen Lord and thus has special authority. This would be eminently true of the very first person to see the risen Jesus. The word "apostle" in the early church often designated those who had this privilege. Thus Paul calls himself an apostle because he had seen the risen Lord (1 Cor 15:9). In 1 Corinthians 9:1 he writes, "Am I not an apostle? Have I not seen Christ the Lord?" The command to go tell others is similar to the command of Jesus to the eleven at the end of Matthew's gospel: "Go, make disciples. . . ." Mary's command to "go" is more like an inner witness for others, especially the twelve. Mary is really the first of all apostles in the gospel of John. The beloved disciple is the first to believe on seeing the empty tomb and *soudarion*. But Mary is the first to believe as a result of the initiative of the risen Christ toward one who so ardently sought him, and, like the beloved disciple, risked her life to be beside Jesus on the cross.

In this way, the fourth gospel reverses another tradition that the risen Jesus first appeared to Peter and the twelve (1 Cor 15:5; Lk 24:34). The emphasis on the latter may be due to the need to emphasize succession to Jesus and authoritative teaching. John's account may be more historical in its emphasis on a woman's witness and internal succession.

To sum up: The portrait of Mary Magdalene in this gospel, inspired by the beloved disciple, gives us further clues: *Mary was a close associate of the beloved disciple as a special witness of the unique events on the cross. Their own close relationship to Jesus was very similar, so much so that Mary is almost a counterpart of the beloved disciple. They were the persons, along with Jesus' mother, who were most closely bound to Jesus. Two people so closely tied to Jesus would certainly be closely associated to one another. The position of the beloved disciple as an inner successor of Jesus is strengthened by the portrait of Mary Magdalene sharing the same role from a woman's unique standpoint. As a result Mary Magdalene becomes an apostle of apostles by being the necessary messenger of Jesus' resurrection to Peter and the other disciples.*

10
A Mystical and Creative Genius

Modern and Ancient Meanings of a Mystic

The word "mystical" deserves an explanation: it is not meant to convey the image of a cross-legged Buddha contemplating the eternal realities. Our sense here will be in accord with the thought-patterns and world view of the gospel writer. Perhaps the best way to bring this out is by way of comparison and contrast with modern scientific views.

Ever since Einstein, a dramatic change has been taking place in our views of the universe. Every school child quickly learns his famous equation $E = MC^2$ which states that all "solid" matter is really composed of unbelievable amounts of invisible energy within atoms and molecules. As Frijof Capra[73] expresses it, "What is *really* out there is a continuous dance of energy. We are living in a vast network of energy, where everything is connected with everything else." This new scientific realization is causing us to reject the mechanistic views of the universe that grew up in past centuries.

Strangely enough, what we know in our *minds* was deeply *felt* by people in the biblical world. They called this interconnected great energy of the universe the Spirit or Breath of God. They experienced its presence in all living beings—plants, trees, animals, human beings—as well as in all the workings of the universe. This mighty Spirit gave all the visible universe life, energy and direction. The breathing process was the great energy process in which all creatures shared. Far from being a dead, mechanistic world, the whole universe was alive and *conscious* with interconnecting patterns of harmony, oneness and direction.

Ancient men and women strove to live in harmony and communion with this great Energy in which everything was connected to everything else. How did they do this? Their secret involved keen observation of the universe based on their deep convictions of interrelatedness. By way of analogy, let us take this example: We are all firmly convinced of the unity of the human person. Even a slight gesture or small intonation of the voice is enough for us to draw conclusions about the intentions, direction and character of a person. Details of clothing—a single button unloosed— can sometimes ring a bell inside us.

This common perception of bodily unity is analogous to ancient views of the oneness and harmony of the universe. It was a universe-body where every detail, movement or happening could contain important messages from other beings and from the great divine Energy of the universe. In fact, even little details were extremely important since the great Energy within was simply "bursting at the seams" to manifest itself in some way, just as the "hidden" passionate love or hatred within a human being waits for an opportunity—sometimes unconsciously—to express itself outwardly.

The people of the Bible sometimes called these significant revelatory details by the name "signs." One type of sign was an unusual series of happenings that pointed to a certainty about what God wanted. For example, Abraham, the father of the Hebrews, sent his servant on a long journey to find a wife for his son Isaac (Gen 24). The servant was anxious to find the right woman, for he knew that God's great plans for Abraham and his people were at stake. So he prayed for an unusual sign: when he arrived at his destination, the woman who would respond to his request for a drink with an added offer to water his ten thirsty camels would surely be the extraordinary woman whom God had chosen. When the servant did arrive and met a young woman who made this unusual response, he was sure that it was a sign from God that she was to be the husband for Abraham's son: "I bowed my head and worshiped the Lord and blessed the Lord, the God of my master Abraham, who had led me by the right way to take the daughter of my master's kinsman for his son" (24:48).

Another form of sign was to look deeply within any event to find the ultimate meaning within. For example, when the devil tempted Jesus to use miraculous powers to provide bread for himself in the desert, Jesus responded by quoting scripture: "Not by bread alone does a person live but by every word that comes from the mouth of God" (Mt 4:4; Dt 8:3). In other words, behind all bread is the Source of all bread and nourishment, the creative word of God. The whole quotation follows:

> He humbled you and let you hunger and fed you with manna, which you did not know, nor did your fathers know; that he might make you know that a person does not live by bread alone, but by everything that proceeds out of the mouth of the Lord.

A third way to perceive a sign was through some happening or detail which revealed God's plan in scripture. For a Jew in the first century, as well as for Christians, these scriptures were filled with hidden meanings which God could reveal to chosen souls. For example, in the book of Daniel, the prophet read the text of Jeremiah which foretold a restoration of the exiles in seventy years (9:2; Jer 25:11; 29:10). Daniel then fasted and prayed for an entire day and asked what the text might mean in his own situation. The angel Gabriel came to him at the time of the evening sacrifice and explained that the text referred to seventy weeks of years and then showed him how it applied to the new crisis faced by the Jewish people. This was the Greek persecution in the second century B.C.E., several centuries after the exile about which Jeremiah had originally spoken. This is what we call a secret or hidden meaning of scripture as revealing God's plan.

Going now to the gospel of John, let us see how the creative and mystical genius of the beloved disciple enables him to perceive the deep meaning of the final events of Jesus' life. We will select some events from the passion account where it is much more clear that the beloved disciple was an actual witness upon whom the author depends.

A Creative and Mystical Genius at Work:
The Passion Account

The passion account in John really begins with the prophetic sign of the washing of the feet in chapter 13. Sandra Schneiders[74] has pointed out that the external washing is not merely a humble act of service, but is a means of entering into the saving effect of Jesus' death. It is "a participation in Jesus' work of transforming the sinful structures of domination operative in human society according to the model of friendship expressing itself in joyful mutual service unto death."[75] The audience is invited to make that sign part of their own lives, as Jesus says:

> You call me Teacher and Lord; and you are right, for so I am.
> If I then, your Lord and Teacher, have washed your feet, you
> also ought to wash one another's feet. For I have given you an
> example, that you also should do as I have done to you
> (13:13–14).

The arrest of Jesus is told with unusual and surprising descriptions (18:1–12): Judas, the soldiers, and the Pharisees seem to represent all the powers of the world as they encounter Jesus. It seems to be an important channel for the believer to enter into a deliberate sign, since Jesus knows all that is to happen to him (18:4). The hesitation of the group to arrest Jesus prompts the beloved disciple and the author to reflect deeply on the meaning of the event as reflected in the scriptures. It all seems to be a fulfillment of the prologue where it is stated that the light has come into the world, but the darkness could not grasp (arrest) him (1:15).

The scriptures in the background appear to be the story of the attempted arrest of the great prophet Elijah by a group of fifty soldiers sent by the king (2 Kgs 1:9–14). The soldiers' captain arrogantly called to Elijah on top of a hill and said, "Man of God, come down." Elijah however answered, "If I am a man of God, let fire come down from heaven and consume you and your fifty." The text then reads, "Then fire came down from heaven, and consumed him and his fifty." The king then sent another band of fifty soldiers and the same result ensued. Finally, the king sent a third group, but this time the captain fell on his knees and humbly asked Elijah to accompany him.

The above story was not intended to be taken seriously in every detail because of the comic play on words in Hebrew. Man (*ish* in Hebrew) of God is very similar in pronunciation to fire (*esh*). However, the sense is clear that no one can really arrest a prophet of God without God's permission. The same is true of Jesus and those believers arrested after him. The power of the divine name (represented by Jesus' words, "I am he") will protect them. So Jesus voluntarily delivers himself over to his arresters with the words, "If you seek me, let these men go" (18:8). The author then notes the significance of Jesus' words as he surrenders himself so that others may be saved: "This was to fulfill the word which he had spoken, 'Of those whom you gave me I lost not one.' "

In the central crucifixion narrative the sign indications are most prominent. Special attention is drawn to the title on the cross (19:22). Pilate himself inscribes it with the words, "Jesus of Nazareth, king of the Jews." The inscription is in a public place where many Jews can see it, and it is written in Hebrew, Latin and Greek. Thus it appears to be a public and universal proclamation by the Roman governor that the messiah truly reigns from the cross. The chief priests therefore went to Pilate and objected to it, saying that it should read instead, "This man said 'I am king of the Jews.' " However, the previously vacillating Pilate now refuses to change it; thus his unusual persistence enhances the sign value.

Next, the dividing of Jesus' garments is singled out as fulfilling the scriptures (19:23–25). The seamless tunic is emphasized:

> The tunic was without seam, woven from top to bottom; so they said to one another, "Let us not tear it, but cast lots for it to see whose it shall be" (19:24).

It has often been claimed that the seamless robe symbolizes the priesthood of Christ because the Jewish high priest wore such a robe and because the risen Christ in the book of Revelation is described as "clothed with a long robe and with a golden girdle round his breast" (1:13). However, I. de la Potterie[76] has carefully examined all these arguments and concluded negatively. Instead, the robe seems to point to the unity of the people of God brought about by Jesus' death. This would be in line with the writer's interpretation of Caiaphas' prediction that it was expedient that one man die for the people. The author notes that the high priest prophesied that Jesus should die for the nation, "and not for the nation only, but to gather into one the children of God who are scattered around" (11:52). It also accords with the theme of unity which we have seen in other places in the gospel. The sign value for the audience would be to commit themselves to the same unity that Jesus died for.

The most important sign is Jesus' actual manner of death and the sign of the blood that follows which we have already studied in the previous chapters. The sign of Mary Magdalene's encounter with the risen Jesus has also been treated in the last chapter. Special attention should also be given to the sign of the *soudarion* which has been brought out by a very perceptive study by S. Schneiders.[77] She defines this as follows: "The face veil is best understood as a Johannine semeion, i.e., as a sign in and through which a properly disposed person can encounter the glory of God revealed in Jesus."[78]

For reference and better understanding, the text follows:

Peter then came out with the other disciple, and they went toward the tomb. They both ran, but the other disciple outran Peter and reached the tomb first; and stooping to look in, he saw the linen cloths lying there, but he did not go in. Then Simon Peter came, following him, and went into the tomb; he saw the linen cloths lying, and the napkin, which had been on his head, not lying with the linen cloths but rolled up in a place by itself. Then the other disciple, who reached the tomb first, also went in, and he saw and believed; for as yet they did not

know the scripture, that he must rise from the dead. Then the
disciples went back to their homes (20:3–10).

Schneiders suggests that the author carefully sets up this sign
as follows. The story of Peter and the beloved disciple at the tomb
is told in great detail (20:2–10) with a very clear beginning and
end. Both disciples are physically together at the beginning and
together in their ignorance of the scriptures at the end. Three
times the beloved disciple's prior arrival at the tomb is mentioned
in verses 4, 6 and 8. Peter, however, first enters the tomb, perhaps
in view of his authority. Peter sees the empty tomb and the burial
cloths, which the beloved disciple had already seen from the outside by stooping down, but not entering (20:5). So neither believes in view of these facts. However, Peter saw something inside
which the beloved disciple had not yet seen: the napkin or face
cloth neatly wrapped up. Yet this does not occasion any belief.
However, the beloved disciple then enters and sees this face veil
for the first time and then does believe. So this *soudarion* must
have special meaning for him.

What meaning then does the *soudarion* or face veil have? Of
course, the carefully wrapped cloth could indicate there was no
grave robbery and be the occasion of the beloved disciple's belief,
although it was not enough for Peter. However, Schneiders makes
the interesting suggestion that the *soudarion* is meant to recall the
face veil Moses used to wear when speaking with God (Ex 34:33–
35). The face veil in the gospel story is not simply dropped or left
as the burial cloths were, but definitely wrapped and put aside.
This recalls Moses' action when he put aside the veil when he
went to speak to God, but then resumed it when he returned to
speak to the people. In regard to Jesus, the new Moses, it would
mean that he has put aside the veil of the flesh and ascended into
the presence of God.

It was this scriptural sign of the veil of Moses that prompted
the beloved disciple to believe. What did he believe? At the end
of the story it is noted that neither disciple as yet understood the
scriptures that Jesus must rise from the dead. This sounds contra-
dictory until we distinguish between Jesus' glorification which

took place when Jesus died, returning to the Father, and his resurrection by which he returns to his own disciples. So Schneiders writes:

> What the face veil reveals is the former, that Jesus, the New Moses, has ascended to God; that he has gone away. This the Beloved Disciple believes. Only with the appearances will it become clear that Jesus has also returned to his own to take up his abode in them, constituting them his presence in the world.[79]

Consequently, the reader is now prepared for what will follow in the next episode about the revelation to Mary Magdalene: that the risen Lord will be where the disciples are gathered together (20:17–18). This prepares the way for the third episode in 20:19–23 where Jesus solemnly breathes the Holy Spirit upon them and transfers to them the same mission that the Father had given him.

To sum up: The author and the beloved disciple are closely linked. The former relies on the eyewitness and the insights of the latter in order to write the story of Jesus, especially the closing events of his life. The way this is done points to the following additional clues about the beloved disciple: *He is a highly gifted, sensitive and creative genius who is most alert to the deep sign value of the actions and events in Jesus' life. In doing so, he shows a highly developed biblical appreciation of the connectedness, harmony and inner direction of God's great energy—the creative Logos—in the universe. He sees this as all brought to completion in Jesus' life and death. What others might see as insignificant details are perceived by him as signs pointing to who Jesus is and what he is to those who believe in him.*

11
The Historicity of the Fourth Gospel Portrait of the Beloved Disciple

Is John's Gospel Less Historical Than Other Gospel Sources?

So far we have used only the fourth gospel as a source in our search for the identity and role of the beloved disciple. What about other sources—the gospels of Mark, Matthew and Luke—which provide most of the information available on the earthly life of Jesus? It would seem that an important person like the beloved disciple would receive some mention in the other three gospels. However, on reading through them, there is nothing on first glance that would indicate a disciple who would be distinct, as we have pointed out, from John the apostle, son of Zebedee. So the first question is whether we should presume that these other three gospels are more historical than John's gospel.

Sometimes it is quickly taken for granted that Matthew, Mark and Luke are more historically oriented than John, which contains so much imagery and symbolism. However, the gospels deal with history in a special sense: their goal is to give their audience the *meaning* of Jesus' life and ministry, especially in view of his death, resurrection and continued presence in believers. They are not interested in furnishing newspaper-type details. The details they do select are in accord with this general purpose as well as with the particular purposes and goals of each gospel. Each gospel, then, is fully historical in this sense. Norman Perrin wrote on this matter of history in the following manner:

So far as we can tell today, there is no single pericope any-
where in the gospels, the present purpose of which is to preserve a historical reminiscence of the earthly Jesus, although
there may be some which do in fact come near to doing so
because a reminiscence, especially of an aspect of teaching
such as a parable, could be used to serve the purpose of the
Church or the evangelist.[80]

In regard to John's gospel, I follow the studies of scholars who
have found that this gospel does contain genuine historical and
independent traditions that are not found in the synoptic gospels.
For example, R.E. Brown concludes:

We do believe that John is based on a solid tradition of the
works and words of Jesus, a tradition which at times is very
primitive. We believe that often John gives us correct historical information about Jesus that no other Gospel has preserved.[81]

J. Louis Martyn in his book *History and Theology in the Fourth
Gospel* reminds us of the importance of historical tradition for the
ancient world:

The past—specific events and teachings of the past—lived on
with power and somehow mingled with events of the present.
To the ancients it was far more obvious than it is to us that
one's response to contemporary issues involves careful consideration of the traditions inherited from one's forebears.[82]

As a result he states, "Consequently, when we read the Fourth
Gospel, we are listening both to tradition and to a new and unique
interpretation of that tradition."[83]

When comparing the synoptic gospels and John's gospel, it is
quite plausible that in some cases the latter preserves some genuine historical reminiscences that the others do not have. This

emerges if we use one criterion of critical historians: that if a source preserves information that is embarrassing or harmful to the authors or their goals, it is likely that this information is true. For example, we would not expect the Pentagon records of the Vietnam War to preserve accounts of mass murders of civilians. So even a hint in their records that such a thing took place should be seriously investigated.

As an example of such embarrassing details, only the fourth gospel tells us that Peter and other members of the twelve were first of all disciples of John the Baptist who introduced them to Jesus (1:35–51). This is omitted by the other gospels. It was something that would furnish valuable arguments to disciples of John the Baptist that their master was indeed prior to Jesus and furnished him with his first disciples. Matthew, Mark and Luke, instead, have Jesus meeting his future apostles for the first time near the Lake of Galilee where he calls them to their future ministry. It would seem that the gospel of John in this case would be more "historical."

In line with this criterion that embarrassing matters preserved in a document are likely to be historical, it should be kept in mind that the fourth gospel description of Jesus' affectionate relationship with a young disciple would have raised many eyebrows in those days, at least in some circles. So this element alone points to the likelihood that this fourth gospel portrait is historical. In other documents, it may have been omitted because of fears that Jesus' relationship with the beloved disciple would be misunderstood.

Would Other Serious Reasons Have Prompted the Others To Omit the Beloved Disciple?

One important goal of the synoptic gospels was to promote the authority of church teachers based on the twelve apostles in order to counteract divergent tendencies within some Christian communities. It would not be in their interests to name or emphasize a disciple apart from the twelve who was so close to Jesus as well as his heir and successor. This emphasis on the twelve and their authority appears as follows: in a narrative similar to the literary succession[84] pattern of Jacob and his twelve sons, Jesus appoints the twelve, gives them his powers and sends them out to continue his work (Mk 3:13–19; 6:7–13; Mt 9:35–10:42).

Matthew emphasizes Jesus' appointment of Peter and the conveyance of the power of the keys (16:13–20). The gospel ends with a solemn command to the eleven to go out to the world and teach others what they have learned from Jesus, with a special guarantee of his continual presence with them. Luke's gospel and the Acts of the Apostles convey the same concern. To stress succession and continuity in the teaching of the twelve, Luke gives their names in his gospel (6:12–16) and then names them again in the story of church beginnings in Acts 2:12–14. The early church is described as formed by the apostles' teaching: "They devoted themselves to the apostles' teaching, and fellowship, to the breaking of bread and the prayers" (2:41).

Along with this emphasis on the twelve, there seems to have been some fears that disciples outside their number might assume their powers. On one occasion, John the apostle appears to be most rigid in that regard:

> John said to him, "Teacher we saw a man casting out demons in your name, and we forbade him (because he was not following us, in some mss), but Jesus said, "Do not forbid him; for no one who does a mighty work in my name will be able soon after to speak evil of me. For he that is not against us is for us" (Mk 9:49–50).

The text seems to refer to a believer in Jesus, for Jesus could hardly condone falsity or hypocrisy. John the apostle appears to be worried about someone else assuming powers that were given to the twelve: "He gave them authority over the unclean spirits" (6:7). The bracketed addition in the above citation of Mark 9:49 very probably is not original and was added to get around the difficulty, but actually makes it worse.

Why Would the Fourth Gospel Omit the Apostles James and John?

In John's gospel the above names are not found at all except in the generic form "the sons of Zebedee" in the so-called gospel appendix in 21:2. Even if chapter 21 was an original part of the gospel the failure to mention their names while having those of other apostles in the same verse seems to be downgrading James and John. A solution of this question may help with valuable clues later on. It is quite possible that we are dealing with a case of "holy" retaliation: you omit me and I omit you! Since James died as a martyr early in church history (Acts 12:2), we must concentrate on John the apostle to see if his omission from the fourth gospel can furnish any clues for our search. Let us begin with the earliest notice in Paul's letter to the Galatians. There we see that Paul went to Jerusalem about fourteen or more (1:18; 2:2) years after his conversion and met with the "pillars" of the church, James (brother of Jesus), Cephas (Peter) and John the apostle (2:9). We note that all three considered their mission limited to the "circumcised," although they agreed to Paul's apostolate to the Gentiles:

> When they perceived the grace that was given to me, James and Cephas and John, who were reputed to be pillars, gave to me and Barnabas the right hand of fellowship, that we should go to the Gentiles and they to the circumcised; only they would have us remember the poor, which very thing I was eager to do (Gal 2:9–10).

The final requirement about a collection for the poor from the Gentiles seems to convey some hesitancy and the need to prove the authenticity of such an apostolate.

The next incident about Peter's visit to Antioch is quite illuminating about the relationship between Jewish and Gentile Christians:

> When Cephas came to Antioch I [Paul] opposed him to his face, because he stood condemned. For before certain men

came from James he ate with the Gentiles; but when they
came he drew back and separated himself, fearing the circum-
cision party (Gal 2:11–12).

The text tells us that Peter was willing to eat with Gentile
Christians when he first came to Antioch, but when Jewish Christians (from James, their leader) came, he no longer did so lest he
disregard the traditional rules of the law about table fellowship
with Gentiles. It can be presumed that John the apostle agreed
with Peter and especially James in these views. P. Achtemeier
observes,

> The willingness of Peter and Barnabas, along with the other
> Jewish Christians, to abide by those restrictions (Gal. 2:12–
> 13), signaled by their withdrawal from table fellowship with
> those who, perhaps under the direct influence of Paul, did
> not, precipitated the split not only between Jewish and Gen-
> tile Christians, but within the Gentile mission itself ("even
> Barnabas," Gal. 2:13b).[85]

Achtemeier further points out that Paul's action at Antioch did
not receive support at Jerusalem similar to what he previously
received on earlier visits (Gal 1:18–24 and 2:1–10). His lack of
support is a sign of continued deterioration of relations between
Gentile and Jewish Christians.

The Acts of the Apostles contains hints of John's (along with
Peter's) hesitation to undertake any kind of broad apostolate to
the Gentiles outside of their mission to the Jews. (The conversion
of the Roman Cornelius and his household by Peter in Acts 10
seems to be an exception and not part of a larger apostolate.)
Philip (not the apostle) does evangelize Samaria. Peter with John
is "sent" by the Jerusalem community to investigate the conversion of these "half-Jews." But their task is more to certify the
genuineness of the Samaritan apostolate than to engage in an
initiative of their own. The growing suspicion of Paul's work
among the Gentiles seems hinted at by the story of his last visit to
Jerusalem. James the brother of the Lord, the community leader,

asks him to submit to Jewish ritual sacrifice for nazirites to prove to Jewish Christians that he respects the law (Acts 21:18–40). When Paul is arrested and imprisoned by Roman authorities, there is no mention of any support for him by the Jewish Christian community.

The gospels of Matthew, Mark and Luke were written long after these events but contain some incidents that deal with the attitudes of John and his brother James. Jesus nicknames them "sons of thunder" (Mk 3:17). This designation is reflected in a Lukan story about the two brothers when Jesus was refused hospitality in a Samaritan town:

> When his disciples James and John saw it, they said, "Lord, do you want us to bid fire come down from heaven and consume them?" But he turned and rebuked them (9:53).

Since the gospel stories often reflect later situations in the church the incident suggests that John and James opposed a Samaritan apostolate, a matter which is very important to the fourth gospel with its detailed story of the Samaritan woman and the enthusiastic reception given to Jesus by Samaritans (4:1–42).

In addition, there is an uncomplimentary story about the two brothers pushing for special places for themselves in a hoped-for Jewish messianic restored kingdom. During the final journey to Jerusalem, when hopes were high, James and John came to Jesus with a special request:

> James and John, the sons of Zebedee, came forward to him, and said to him, "Teacher, we want you to do for us whatever we ask of you." And he said to them, "What do you want me to do for you?" And they said to him, "Grant us to sit, one at your right hand and one at your left, in your glory" (Mk 10:35–37).

In response, Jesus had to correct their ideas and emphasize the necessity of suffering in order to be part of the coming kingdom. The story notes that the boldness of the sons of Zebedee made the other ten apostles angry: "When the other ten heard it, they began to be indignant at James and John" (10:41). The event is so embarrassing that Matthew softens it by having their mother make the request for them (20:20–21)! Luke goes even further and omits it entirely. This expectation of a restored kingdom of Israel also appears in the Acts of the Apostles when the apostles question Jesus: "Lord, will you at this time restore the kingdom to Israel?" (1:6).

Other reasons also may have dictated these "reciprocal omissions" of the fourth gospel and synoptics. The latter concentrate their attention on Jesus' activity and ministry in Galilee. This was his home territory and that of the twelve. In contrast, the fourth gospel is centered about Judea and draws its inspiration from the beloved disciple who is from that area. He appears to have relatively little acquaintance with Galilee except for the few cities and incidents he records.

Putting together the above information, it is easier to understand why the fourth gospel so neatly omitted John and James. James became a martyr early in church history (Acts 12:2), and our texts show John's exclusive commitment to an apostolate to the circumcised, as well as opposition to a Samaritan apostolate. He also seemed to be an advocate of the restoration of the kingdom in terms of Jewish nationalistic hopes. All of these views are directly contrary to the fourth gospel. This gospel shows a very special interest in a Samaritan apostolate in the story of Jesus' encounter with a Samaritan woman and his subsequent enthusiastic reception in Samaria (4:1–42). Far from being a nationalistic messiah in the gospel of John, Jesus is the lamb of God who takes away the sins of the *world* (1:29). This whole world, *cosmos,* also comes into other prominent gospel texts, e.g. Jesus is the "savior of the world" (4:42) and "God so loved the world that he gave his only Son" (3:16). In addition, John's gospel does not foster any kind of divisive spirit between Jewish and Gentile Christians. We have already seen that a central gospel theme is oneness: "one flock and one shepherd" (10:16). Jesus dies to "gather into one the children of God who are scattered abroad" (11:52).

12
Clues to the Beloved Disciple
in the Synoptic Gospels

First of all, by way of general atmosphere, we note the prominence of children and young people in these gospels through the frequent use of the Greek word *paidion,* child, or young person. Outside the infancy stories, the word is found some thirty-six times. It does not necessarily refer to a small child. The "child" of Jairus is twelve years old (Mk 5:42). Jesus uses this word to mean "young men" in the story of the miraculous draught of fish when he calls out to his disciples, "Children, have you any fish?" (Jn 21:5). This wide range follows the biblical usage where the word can refer to a child, a young person, or a servant. The young Benjamin is called a *paidion* eight times in Genesis 43. Joseph, a seventeen year old youth, is described by a similar, parallel word, *paidarion* (Gen 37:30; 42:22).

In the gospels, Jesus' fondness for children, his popularity with them and his frequent teaching references to them are well illustrated. He spends time with them, delighting to touch, bless and embrace them (Mk 10:13–16; 9:36). To scandalize a little one is the most horrible of sins (9:42). To receive a child is to receive Jesus himself (9:37). To illustrate which people have first place in the kingdom, Jesus takes a child in his arms in front of the twelve (9:35). Only those who become humble like children can enter the kingdom of God (Mt 18:1–4). Watching children's games can teach important lessons (11:16–17). When Jesus entered the temple on his final visit to Jerusalem it was children who publicly acclaimed him as messiah, crying out, "Hosanna to the Son of David." Even when the chief priests and scribes asked Jesus to silence them, he refused to do so. In response, he quoted scripture that God's word is proclaimed by children and infants (Mt 21:15–36).

Mark and the Young Spiritual Successors of Jesus (9:33–37; 10:13–16)

These unusual and similar stories about children have not been given the attention they deserve. The first follows Jesus' second prediction about his coming suffering, death and resurrection. Then the narrative describes the disciples arguing on the way about who would be greatest in the coming kingdom. With the mention of Jesus' death, the gospel audience would naturally think about Jesus' successors in that kingdom. So Jesus' response in this matter is especially important:

> He sat down and called the twelve; and he said to them, "If anyone would be first, he must be last of all and servant of all." And he took a child, and put him in the midst of them; and taking him in his arms, he said to them, "Whoever receives one such child in my name receives me; and whoever receives me, receives not me but him who sent me" (9:33–37).

We note specific mention of *the twelve,* and then Jesus' emphasis on the youngster placed in their midst as if in contrast to the twelve, who had just been arguing about who would be the greatest. J.M. Derrett[86] has shown that the words, "taking him in his arms," are similar to those used in adoption scenes in the Old Testament, especially where Jacob adopts the two sons of Joseph as his very own in Genesis 48:8–15 by embracing them (taking them into his arms). Thus Jesus takes the lad in his arms in a ritual symbolizing that a child is his true successor in contrast to the ambitious twelve. The contrast to the twelve is made even stronger in the following incident where John the apostle (no less) forbids the exercise of power by someone outside the twelve and receives a sharp rebuke from Jesus (9:38–42).

The succession motif above is confirmed by Jesus' words about the youngster, "Whoever receives one such child in my name receives me; and whoever receives me, receives not me but him who sent me" (9:37). These words clearly express identification of the one sent (the child) with the one sending (Jesus and God). The same mission expression is used of the twelve in Jesus' special instruction to them in Matthew 10:40. They are also found in the last supper in John 13 as part of Jesus' commission and last instructions to his disciples, an occasion where the beloved disciple is singled out as a successor of Jesus (13:20).

Mark highlights Jesus' symbolic gesture toward the youngster by repeating elements in the story in another similar account:

> They were bringing children to him, that he might touch them; and the disciples rebuked them. But when Jesus saw it he was indignant, and said to them, "Let children come to me, do not hinder them; for to such belongs the kingdom of God. Truly, I say to you, whoever does not receive the kingdom of God like a child shall not enter it." And he took them in his arms and blessed them, laying his hands upon them (Mk 10:13–16).

The common elements with the preceding story are striking, making us think that Mark has made a deliberate literary frame or *inclusio* from the two accounts. The acute conflict with the twelve is again evident. They had just experienced such great difficulty with Jesus' teaching on divorce that he had to repeat it to them in the house (10:10). Then they try to keep the women from bringing children to Jesus and provoke his strong rebuke. In both stories Jesus takes the children into his arms in a symbolic action of adoption. In addition, in the second story, Jesus "blessed them, laying his hands on them." A special blessing was part of the ritual of adoption and successorship in the Old Testament as seen in Jacob's blessing for his twelve sons, his special adoption blessing for Joseph's sons, and in Moses' blessing of the twelve tribes (Gen 49:28; 48:20; Dt 33:1).

A few other notes on the above text: Jesus' gesture for the children seems to have happened frequently since the Greek imperfect tense signifies a continued or repeated past action. The affectionate nature of his action is shown by the words, "He took them in his arms and blessed them, laying his hands upon them" (10:16). This implies taking them on his lap, or on his bosom (like the beloved disciple in John 13:23). This action would be necessary if he were to lift up his hands for a blessing (cf. Lk 24:50) and then place his hands on their heads.

The unusual affection of Jesus for young ones can be seen by examining the parallels in Matthew and Luke who seem to feel it should be toned down. Matthew makes it into a solitary occasion by changing the Greek to a past tense rather than the imperfect: "Children were brought to him that he might lay his hands on them and pray." Matthew also omits the marks of affection such as taking them in his arms and touching them that we saw in Mark (Mt 19:13–15). Luke makes the incident even more acceptable by changing the "children" into infants (Greek, *brephe),* and likewise omitting the marks of affection (18:15–17). Perhaps there was some embarrassment about Jesus' very evident affection for youngsters.

We can also observe in the first story that a particular child or youngster is singled out. Since the incident took place at Jesus' home in Capernaum, it would be likely that Jesus knew him. The lesson to the twelve is clear: the *paidion* occupies the important place by Jesus that they themselves coveted. The taking of the child into the arms or bosom parallels the scene in John 13 where the beloved disciple at the bosom of Jesus is a counterpart to Peter and the others (13:20). In the fourth gospel, Capernaum seems to be the Galilean town the writer is most familiar with, mentioned three times (2:12; 4:46; 6:17). Matthew omits the above scene entirely. Luke shortens it and omits the signs of affection, but heightens the position of the "child" by writing, "He took a child and put him at his side." He also adds the saying, "He who is least among you all is the one who is great" (9:47–48).

All in all, the story fits in well with description of the beloved disciple in the supper scene of John 13. As adopted son (in the fourth gospel), the beloved disciple would certainly know Jesus' special home in Capernaum. Thus, if he were there at the time, he would be the logical youngster for Jesus to call upon to illustrate his teachings about the first place in the kingdom. Jesus usually confirmed his sayings with actions. In this case, he illustrated who was first in the kingdom of God by keeping a "child" at the privileged place by his side or at his bosom.

It is also remarkable that Mark alone in his gospel preserves the tradition that a certain young man, not one of the twelve, continued to follow Jesus even after the rest of his disciples fled after the master's arrest:

> A young man followed him with nothing but a linen cloth about his body; and they seized him, but he left the linen cloth and ran away naked (14:51–52).

This accords with the story in John's gospel that the young beloved disciple (not one of the twelve) continued to follow Jesus even though Peter and presumably the others deserted him (18:15–18). In addition, the same[87] young man of Mark 14:51–52 also appears in that gospel's climax as the one who announces Jesus' resurrection to the women and gives them the commission to bring the news to Peter and the others (16:5–7). Thus he is the first believer in Jesus' resurrection, just as the beloved disciple is the first to believe on entering the tomb of Jesus: "Then the other disciple, who reached the tomb first, also went in, and he saw and believed" (Jn 20:12).

The Lukan and Johannine Last Suppers

The Lukan version of the last supper has remarkable similarities to that in John and forms a valuable link to the prominent beloved disciple in that account. The pertinent text in Luke follows:

> A dispute also arose among them, which of them was to be regarded as the greatest. And he said to them, "The kings of

the Gentiles exercise lordship over them; and those in authority over them are called benefactors. But not so with you;
rather let the greatest among you become as the youngest, and
the leader as one who serves. For which is the greater, one
who sits at table, or one who serves? But I am among you as
one who serves (Lk 22:24–27).

What Luke describes by *word* in his account is *acted out* in
John's last supper story. Luke has Jesus say that the true leader is
one who serves, in opposition to the common view that it is one
who sits at table being served: "I am among you as one who
serves." In John, Jesus acts this out by washing the feet of his
disciples, just as a servant might do. There is also a similarity in
the "lord" expressions. In Luke, the contrast is between those
who "lord it over" the others, and the attitude of humble service.
In John, the word "Lord" is stressed by a fourfold repetition
(13:6, 9, 13, 14). Peter emphasizes the contrast when he protests
about Jesus' foot-washing: "Lord, do *you* wash *my* feet?" (13:6).
At the end of the foot-washing Jesus explains his own action as an
example for every disciple to follow:

> You call me Teacher and Lord; and you are right, for so I am.
> If I then, your Lord and Teacher, have washed your feet, you
> also ought to wash one another's feet. For I have given you an
> example, that you also should do as I have done to you
> (13:13–15).

Within this general similarity of Luke and John, especially
significant is the dispute in Luke about who was the greatest.
Such a conflict would quite naturally concern itself about the
special places near Jesus at such an important banquet. There is a
similar situation in Jesus' banquet parable where the guests try to
seize the first places (Lk 14:7–11). Jesus tells them at the last
supper, "Let the greatest among you become as the youngest and
the leader as one who serves" (Lk 22:26).

It is also interesting to note in our parallels to Joseph in the
Old Testament that his story begins with a description of his place

in the family as the youngest son and especially beloved of Jacob because he is the child of his father's old age (Gen 37:3).

We can conclude from the comparison between the two supper scenes that there are many close links between them and some clues that the beloved disciple may have been associated with the Lukan supper. If so, why is he not explicitly named? A possible explanation is that the apostolic orientation of the synoptic gospels could not allow this. This is especially true of the supper scene where the twelve dominate. In Mark, Jesus came to the supper "with the twelve" (14:17). It is "one of the twelve" who will betray him (14:19). Matthew's account is similar (26:20). In Luke, the place of the twelve is most prominent of all: the apostles John and James are sent to make the preparations (22:8). The word *sent* may imply a certain authority in regard to the meal. Jesus sits at the table "and the apostles with him" (22:8). The twelve are promised places at the future kingdom banquet table where they will judge the *twelve* tribes of Israel (22:28–30). We would not expect a direct mention of the beloved disciple, rather than of the twelve, as holding the first place at the supper. It simply would not go along with Luke's apostolic emphasis in his gospel, especially in regard to the last supper. There may also be a question of apostolic interpretation of the breaking of the bread. The "teaching of the apostles" and the "breaking of bread" are mentioned together in Luke's second volume, Acts 2:42.

To sum up: It cannot be said that the fourth gospel is less "historical" than the other three. Omissions and insertions are largely governed by the purposes of each gospel. The synoptic gospels have a heavy "apostolic" orientation and would be likely to omit disciples such as the beloved disciple who was outside the circle of the twelve. On the other hand, the fourth gospel with its interior emphasis, and broad interest in Samaritan and Gentile apostolates, would be likely to play down or omit those members of the twelve (such as James and John) whose outlook was much more confining, or even opposed to such a new direction.

Despite these differences, some clues about the beloved disciple emerge from the gospels of Matthew, Mark and Luke. *Jesus' special interest and affection for children and young people, not*

*just in general but in particular, is strongly affirmed. This is espe-
cially true of the incident in Jesus' Capernaum home where a
known youngster was embraced and placed at Jesus' side as an
example, as well as in contrast to the apostles in their argument
over first places near Jesus. Mark's gospel also preserves the tradition that there was a mysterious young man and close disciple of
Jesus outside of the twelve who kept following him even when Peter
and the others had fled. Like the beloved disciple he was present at
the empty tomb and was the first to believe in the resurrection of
Jesus. The Lukan and Johannine suppers have remarkable similarities in Jesus' words about first places at table and humble service.
The conflict theme between lordship and loving service is in both
gospels. Finally, Jesus states that the youngest, like the Old Testament Joseph, should be in the first place as an example of role
reversal and service. This would be especially meaningful if the
beloved disciple were actually present. His literary omission may
be explained by the heavy apostolic domination of the last supper,
especially in Luke.*

13
Putting Together the Clues:
A Composite Portrait of the Beloved Disciple

Putting together all our clues (strong and weak!), we arrive at the following composite portrait of the beloved disciple. He was certainly not John, son of Zebedee and one of the twelve. As a young lad he met Jesus by the Jordan River with John the Baptist, whose close disciple and protégé he had been. The beloved disciple was from Judea, probably Jerusalem. He was perhaps a member of a priestly family, and was well known at the high priest's household in Jerusalem. During the time John and Jesus were together by the Jordan, a deep bond of teacher/disciple grew up between the two. Jesus adopted the youngster as his own son in a strong affectionate relationship.

It does not seem that John stayed continually with Jesus in Galilee. However, when John visited Galilee, their close relationship was apparent, especially when they were together in Jesus' new home in Capernaum. At such times Jesus gave him a first place by his side in a way that aroused the jealousy of other apostles, especially James and John. However, Jesus insisted that the close presence of such a "child" was a public example of spiritual childhood and of the reversal of the typical human patterns of domination and authority. Jesus' affectionate relationship to the beloved disciple, children and young people was a source of friction as well as embarrassment to the chosen twelve who saw John as a threat to their own special position.

The beloved disciple was especially close to Jesus during his final stay in Judea and Jerusalem. There at the last supper, he held a privileged place at Jesus' bosom. He was first to know Jesus' profound secret of his coming betrayal and death. Modeling himself on the Old Testament Joseph, the beloved disciple came to see himself as an inner successor to Jesus with a mission to bring a deep understanding of Jesus' life and especially his death to the world. This was in counterpart to Peter and the twelve who were outer successors in regard to authority and apostolate.

When Jesus was arrested, all the twelve fled except John who followed the master as far as the cross. Peter arrived, with John's help, within the courtyard of the high priest where he denied that he even knew the master. The central moments in the beloved disciple's life were at the foot of the cross where he gained a remarkable insight into the meaning of Jesus' death. It was the seventh sign especially—the flow of watery blood from Jesus' side—that eventually made him understand the priestly nature of Jesus' death as a new passover lamb and source of the Spirit. In the course of time, he saw its connection to the fourth sign of the loaves and the difficult saying of Jesus about eating his flesh and drinking his blood.

John's association with Jesus' mother and Mary Magdalene were key influences in his life, especially the unforgettable time they shared at the foot of the cross. He understood and fulfilled Jesus' final wish to continue the relationship of favorite son through an act of adoption on the part of Jesus' mother. The association with Jesus' mother and their life together became the source of many insights for him, especially in regard to the first sign of Cana as the completion and continuation of the seventh sign at the cross. Jesus' last testament in regard to his mother and the beloved disciple gave him a special credential and authorization to convey to others a new and deep understanding of Jesus' mission in view of his "hour."

In regard to Mary Magdalene, John understood her close link to Jesus and portrayed her close covenant relationship with Jesus after his resurrection. John saw her as a chosen "apostle to apostles" to bring the first news of Jesus' resurrection to others. He saw her as his own counterpart in being an authentic witness and inner successor to Jesus.

The gospel clues, especially the beloved disciple's perceptive interpretation of signs, reveal to us the portrait of an unusual and gifted young man. He was a true poet and artist, deeply sensitive to Jesus' inner life as well as to the people and events around him. His own affectionate relationship to Jesus prompted him to interpret Jesus' whole mission in terms of love and service. His position as inner successor to Jesus enabled him to understand the priority of the Spirit working in him and in others. He saw this Spirit as the real successor and double of Jesus continuing his presence and work in each new generation. While Peter and external successors were part of this work, their role was to be in subordination and service to that Spirit.

A Note on This Close and Affectionate Male Relationship

While modern readers may find this relationship surprising it is by no means unusual in the Bible. For example, the Hebrew King David's closest friend was Jonathan, the son of his rival Saul. The Bible describes their relationship as follows:

> The soul of Jonathan was knit to the soul of David, and Jonathan loved him as his own soul. . . . Then Jonathan made a covenant with David, because he loved him as his own soul (1 Sam 18:1).

As regards teacher–disciple relationships, the Hebrew prophet Elisha had a protégé, a boy called Gehazi. He seems to have been an understudy of the prophet who was training him to be a successor. He employed him on important tasks such as to raise up the son of a widow (2 Kgs 4:29). In the New Testament, Paul took the young Timothy with him on his journeys. As time went on, Timothy became more and more attached to Paul as a beloved disciple, favorite son and finally his own successor (Acts 16:2; 1 Cor 4:17; 2 Tim 1:3–6).

Such close male relationships were accompanied by customary marks of affection such as kisses or embraces. The kiss of Judas was selected as a means of identifying Jesus at his arrest because such a kiss was an ordinary sign of greeting between close friends or between disciple and master (Mk 14:44; Mt 26:48; Lk 22:47). These expressions were part of a biblical cultural pattern in which physical demonstrations of affection were considered much more acceptable. For example, David and Jonathan kissed one another on taking farewell (1 Sam 20:41); as king, David kissed and blessed the old man Barzillai before sending him home. In Luke's gospel, Jesus rebuked his Pharisee host Simon who gave him no welcome kiss, and contrasted him to the penitent woman who showered kisses on his feet while he was at table (7:45).

Consequently, we find biblical examples confirming that the close male relationship between Jesus and his beloved disciple was much more acceptable and appreciated in ancient times. They took place in a society and environment where *touch* was considered a much more important element in expressing human relationships than in many modern societies. Today, it must be admitted that societies which are non-demonstrative of affection—where people become "untouchable"—are often characterized by an unfortunately high level of violence.

14
The Eclipse of the Beloved Disciple and His Significance Today

An eclipse is a temporary darkening of the earth due to an obstruction of the sun's rays. What happened after the death of our beloved disciple may be termed an eclipse because his extraordinary genius and insights became obscured. Along with other causes, the gospel author, although a faithful disciple or "moon" reflecting the sun rays of his master, sometimes got in the way and caused a temporary darkening. The following are some of the ways by which the eclipse of the beloved disciple happened.

The Apostolic "Appendix" of the Gospel (Chapter 21)

I place "appendix" in quotation marks because scholars have often considered it to be an addition to the gospel after an original ending in 20:31 with these words:

> Now Jesus did many other signs in the presence of the disciples which are not written in this book; but these are written that you may believe that Jesus is the Christ, the Son of God, and that believing you may have life in his name.

However, among others, Paul Minear[88] has presented good reasons to believe that chapter 21 forms an integrated literary part of the gospel as designed by the author. Whether it was or not, this chapter seems to contradict, or at least balance, statements or positions made in the rest of the gospel.

The first story in chapter 21 is the miraculous draught of fish (1–11). It is remarkably similar to the story in Luke 5:1–11 and is probably drawn from the same source. Simon Peter clearly dominates the scene. He invites the disciples to "go fishing," and they agree to go with him. On recognizing the Lord, he throws himself in the sea to come to Jesus. This action reflects another story in Matthew where Peter tries to walk over the sea to come to Jesus (14:28–33). It is Peter who drags the net onto the shore with its one hundred and fifty-three fish whose symbolism has puzzled scholars for almost twenty centuries. The story brings out Peter's preeminence as an apostle and "fisher of men" as in the Lukan parallel (5:10). The beloved disciple is a decidedly secondary though important figure who actually recognizes Jesus first and tells Peter about it (21:7). Even the Zebedees (whose names are strangely omitted) appear for the first and last time in the gospel as fishing companions of Peter (21:1). Thus the tables are turned in chapter 21 from the rest of the gospel where Peter is definitely in second place to the beloved disciple.

In a second apparition, Jesus prepares a meal and eats it with them (9–14). Here everyone recognizes Jesus in his characteristic action of taking bread and fish and giving it to them. Again Peter takes first place. Jesus invites him to bring some of the fish and Peter obeys his command. This stands in contrast to the beloved disciple's first position at the last supper along with his presentation and explanation of the loaves and fish in the fourth sign (6:8ff).

The next scene has a very definite succession motif as Jesus tells Simon Peter three times to feed his sheep (just as Jesus has just fed them?). Jesus himself was the first shepherd in 10:14 when he said: "I am the good shepherd; I know my own and my own know me." Peter's triple repetition of "You *know* I love you" may be related to that text. Peter then is to succeed Jesus in this shepherding role. This shepherd succession theme is confirmed in the story of Moses and Joshua, his successor as leader of Israel. Moses prays that God may appoint someone to take his place and (like a shepherd) go out and come in among them, lead them out and bring them in "that the congregation of the Lord be not as sheep without a shepherd" (Num 27:17–18). The same phrase is used by Jesus in the apostolic succession[89] narrative where he appoints the twelve to continue on after him in the same manner that the twelve sons of Israel succeeded their father (Mt 9:36–10:5). Since Peter has long been dead at the time of this writing, this succession role must have been important for "apostolic" communities as they traced their authoritative teachers back to Peter.

The next scene, a prophetic description of Peter's martyrdom, completes the shepherd theme as he finally becomes like Jesus the good shepherd who lays down his life for his sheep (10:11). The story forms a "rehabilitation" of Peter who will make up for his unfulfilled promise to lay down his life for the master at the last supper scene (13:37). Following this he had denied that he even knew Jesus in the courtyard of the high priest and did not follow him to the cross. So the prediction ends with Jesus' words, "Follow me" (21:19). Thus Peter is effectively brought up to the level of the beloved disciple who followed Jesus to the cross and never denied him.

Another reversal of Peter's role forms the final scene. In the gospel, the revealer of secrets was "the beloved disciple who had lain close to his (Jesus') breast at the supper and had said, 'Lord, who is it that is going to betray you?' " (21:20). Now in contrast, Peter goes ahead and "John" follows: "Peter turned and saw following them the disciple whom Jesus loved." Peter is now the one who asks a special secret from Jesus instead of the beloved disciple at the last supper. He asks Jesus, "What about this man?"

All in all, chapter 21 is a striking reversal to the rest of the gospel. Peter the external successor to Jesus comes out in first place while the beloved disciple as inner successor finishes a weak second. Perhaps pressures from "apostolic" Christians prompted the author to do this after the death of his own teacher the beloved disciple. In making this apostolic emphasis, the author made use of existing stories about Peter into which he brought the beloved disciple.

The Continued Eclipse: The Letters of John

The balance of modern scholarship[90] leans in the direction that these letters, because of their differences in style and content, were not written by the author of the fourth gospel and that they were written after it. They seem to form another step in the eclipse of the beloved disciple. The modern scholar who has perhaps spent the most time in studying the Johannine literature through his masterful trilogy of Anchor Bible Commentaries is Raymond E. Brown. There seems to be a tinge of sadness when he writes as follows in his preface to the volume on the epistles of John:

> It is precisely on the issue of love that we encounter the great anomaly in the Johannine Epistles. The most eloquent NT author on the necessity of love is singularly unloving in dealing with those who disagree with him.[91]

Yet despite this, Brown goes on to plead that the letters only achieve their significance together with the gospel, not apart from it. They witness a struggle within the Johannine community in regard to exaggerated interpretations of the fourth gospel. The arguments in these letters are against "secessionists" influenced by gnostic and docetic views about Jesus. These ideas so emphasized Jesus' divinity and the divinization of believers that Jesus' humanity, the need for forgiveness of sins, and the ethical aspects of love were de-emphasized. The author of the letters felt that these ideas threatened the heart of Christian belief and vehemently fought against them. Unfortunately (as often happens in countering extremes), the author moved so far in the opposite direction that he cast a shadow on the insights of the beloved disciple (in whose name he seemed to be writing).

The following are some definite areas of conflict with the lofty attitudes of the fourth gospel. First, the gospel has a beautiful and sensitive concern for oneness in the midst of diversity. Jesus wants to give his life for all as a good shepherd, including "other sheep not of the fold" that there may be "one flock, one shepherd" (10:16). His final prayer is for oneness in the community: "That they may all be one, even as you, Father, are in me, that they may be one in us, that the world may believe that you have sent me" (17:21). The purpose of his sacrificial death is to achieve oneness: "To gather into one the children of God who are scattered abroad" (11:52).

In contrast to this loving concern for "outsiders" in the gospel, we find the following attitudes of the letters toward Christians of other views as summed up by R.E. Brown:

> He vilifies the opponents who had been members of his own Community as demonic Antichrists, false prophets, and liars (2:18–22; 4:1–6; II John 7) who should not be allowed through the door or even receive ordinary greetings (II John 10). Indeed, their sin is so deadly that one should not even pray about it (I John 5:16–17).[92]

In all fairness, such statements in the letters must be understood in the context of what their author considers a life-death struggle for the preservation of Jesus' authentic teaching. The polemic is characterized by the black and white antithesis of opponents in a bitter struggle. Yet such statements, unfortunately, often fan the flames feeding terrible crusades against unbelievers as well as cruel persecution of "heretics." The logical sequence to "dangerous, devil-inspired, unwanted and unloved" often leads to death.

A second area of marked difference is regarding the Holy Spirit. John's gospel is centered about the Spirit as the continuation of Jesus' presence in his disciples. It begins with the Baptist's vision of the Spirit descending on Jesus and the promise of one who will baptize with the Holy Spirit (1:33–34). It ends with the solemn inauguration of the reign of the Spirit when the risen Jesus breathes on the disciples and says, "Receive the Holy Spirit" (20:23). In contrast, the *Holy* Spirit is not found at all in the letters. Where Jesus had promised in the gospel "another Paraclete" as a "second self" to abide with his disciples, the letters give this title only to Jesus himself (1 Jn 2:1). Most of the spirit references there do not have the personal quality of those in the gospel. Instead, more emphasis is placed on "discretion of spirits." For example, "Brethren, do not believe every spirit, but test the spirits to see whether they are of God" (1 Jn 4:1). Also, "By this you know the Spirit of God: every spirit which confesses that Jesus Christ has come in the flesh is of God" (1 Jn 4:2).

A third area is the abiding presence of God through Jesus. We have touched on the theme of Jesus as the new temple from the opening lines of the gospel: "The Word became flesh and pitched his tent among us" (1:14). Jesus then invites his first disciples to come abide with him, and they respond to his call by staying with him (1:40). This abiding theme goes through the whole gospel. Jesus abides with his disciples through the bread of life (6:56) and continually through the Holy Spirit (chapters 14–16) with such beautiful expressions as, "On that day you will know that I am in my Father, and you in me and I in you" (14:20).

In contrast, the epistles of John seem wary of the experience of direct mystical union with Jesus. All kinds of conditions are attached to make sure it is genuine. Conformity with commandments is mentioned some eleven times. External works of charity are presented as a better guarantee of God's abiding presence than inner experience (3:17–18). In addition, a correct credal statement also certifies God's inner presence: "Whoever confesses that Jesus is the Son of God, God abides in him" (1 Jn 4:15). There is also very little about seeing God in Jesus, or about union with Jesus.

In the gospel, this abiding presence of God or Jesus was a very present and meaningful experience. However, in the letters, the emphasis is more on the future. For example, the author writes, "And now, little children, abide in him, so that when he appears we may have confidence and not shrink from him at his coming" (1 Jn 2:28). Also, "Beloved, we are God's children now; it does not yet appear what we shall be, but we know that when he appears we shall be like him, for we shall see him as he is" (3:2). In fact, there appears to be a whole shift to the future in the letters. None of the beautiful sign-making or mystical qualities so characteristic of the gospel appear.

The Last Phase of the Eclipse

The final step was the progressive identification of the beloved disciple (and gospel author in ancient times) with John the apostle, brother of James and son of Zebedee. This brought "our disciple" into the ring of the twelve. Consequently, the opposition became blurred between the beloved disciple's inner succession to Jesus and the outer succession of the twelve. As part of the twelve, the beloved disciple became part of the authority structure of the church which could interpret the inner, mystical statements in conformity with the teachings of external authority.

The "last blow" was the additional identification of the author and beloved disciple with John, the fiery apocalyptic preacher and author of the book of Revelation (1:9). While there are some correspondences between the gospel and the book of Revelation of John, it is hard to imagine two books so diametrically opposed: the central theme of the gospel is love, with rewards and punishments hardly mentioned. In contrast, rewards and punishments dominate the book of Revelation, especially the image of the fiery pool of boiling sulphur as representing God's eternal punishment (14:10–11; 19:11; 20:14; 21:8).

The End of the Eclipse and the Emergence of the Sun

The end result of the eclipse of the beloved disciple turns out to be a surprise: as a result of the gospel appendix, the letters, and the misidentification with John the apostle, the book inspired by the beloved disciple was considered "safe" enough to be received into the canon of the official books of the church. If the eclipse had not occurred, the beloved disciple's work might have been permanently lost or reduced to a part of the unapproved apocryphal New Testament literature gathering dust in large tomes. As a result, the beloved disciple's work has remained with us. His illuminating sun is no longer in eclipse but continually breaking through the surrounding clouds and fog banks to give light, inspiration and hope to the world.

In closing this book, I am reminded of a namesake and double of the beloved disciple, John XXIII, who was elected pope in 1958. He was hardly in office for ninety days, when on January 25, 1959 he surprised the world by calling an ecumenical council of the whole church. On one occasion, it is said that he was asked why he would do such an extraordinary thing. In reply, he walked over to a window, pulled it open and responded, "To let some fresh air into the church!"

Pope John literally "inspired" the church in accord with the Greek etymology of the word "inspire," meaning to "breathe into." He breathed into the council and church the inner emphasis on the breath/Spirit of God that was so characteristic of John, the beloved disciple and his own namesake. It is my hope that this book will also do its part in bringing out the inner message of the fourth gospel—and of course making the beloved disciple better known and appreciated instead of simply "anonymous."

Notes

(Full information on books and articles will be found in the Bibliography)

1. Pp. 122–123.
2. For a survey of the dating problem, cf. Brown, 1966, pp. lxxx – lxxxiii.
3. The texts in question are not direct quotations but the material is characteristic of Johannine thought.
4. While Justin does write about the Logos, or Word (as only in John), there is not enough to make us certain he is drawing from that gospel.
5. In his apology to Autolycus (ca. 180).
6. Cf. the text of Papias in chapter 2 of this book.
7. For information on this gnostic commentary on John, cf. Elaine Pagels, *The Johannine Gospel in Gnostic Exegesis.*
8. The authorship of these letters is a complex problem. After reviewing all the evidence, Brown, 1982 leans in favor of the evidence that the author of the letters is distinct from the author of the fourth gospel (pp. 19–35).
9. Pp. lxxxvii–xcviii.
10. P. 34.
11. This is the whole argument of his article on the son of Zebedee.
12. P. 43.
13. Chapter 9 will show how the author has transformed the Bethany anointing. For another view, based on the priority of John's gospel, cf. J.F. Coakley. However, the thesis of the priority of John has received the support of very few scholars.
14. For example, P. Ellis based his commentary on the literary

analysis of John Gerhard, which finds that all twenty-one chapters of the gospel form a definite literary pattern. J. Staley has suggested that the gospel prologue provides an outline for a unified literary structure of the whole gospel. While many scholars have regarded chapter 21 as a later appendix, P. Minear has made a rather convincing study to show that it forms a definite part of the original writing. (Cf. his article in the *Journal of Biblical Literature.*)

15. Esp. pp. 33–41.

16. Cf. Bibliography.

17. Cf. Bibliography.

18. The translations of Eusebius below are adapted from the *Fathers of the Church, The Apostolic Fathers.*

19. Pp. 376–377, Eusebius, Hist. Eccl. III,39.

20. *Idem,* p. 375, Irenaeus, Haer V. 33,3.4.

21. *Idem,* p. 387, Jerome, De Vir. Illust. 18 (Migne, PL 23.670).

22. Cf. note 20.

23. References are from Brown, 1966, p. xciv.

24. *Ibid.*

25. *Gemeinde und Gemeindeordnung in Neue Testament.* Zurich, 1959. Reference is from O'Grady, p. 61.

26. Cf. Brown, 1979, p. 31.

27. Culpepper, *Anatomy of the New Testament,* p. 4.

28. *Ibid.,* p. 47.

29. Cf. Brown, 1979, p. 31.

30. Brown, 1979, summarizes the views of the following scholars in his appendix (pp. 171–176): J. Louis Martyn, Georg Richter, Oscar Cullmann, M. Boismard, W. Langbrandtner.

31. Brown, 1979, has summary charts on pp. 165–170 of his hypothesis of the composition of these various groups.

32. Cf. Bibliography.

33. Brown, 1979, p. 197.

34. The journey of Jacob is not difficult to study from this aspect since it is an important example of the literary itinerary genre in the Old Testament. For a study of this genre, see R. A. Bascom.

35. J. Neyrey, "The Jacob Allusions in John 1:51."

36. *Som* i, 68–70.

37. Cf. Bibliography.

38. Cf. Bibliography.

39. Cf. Bibliography.

40. *Targum Pseudo-Jonathan* on Gen 28 to 35.

41. *Old Testament Pseudegrapha,* Vol. 2, 40lff.

42. *Jub.* 32:20. Translations of *Jubilees* are those of O.S. Wintermute in *OTP,* Vol. 2, 35–142.

43. *Tg. Ps.-Jn.,* Gen 35:13.

44. *Tg. Onq.,* Gen 35:13.

45. J. Neyrey, "Jacob Traditions . . ."

46. *Jub.* 32:26.

47. *Jub.* 32:3–7.

48. *Jub.* 32:16.

49. *Jub.* 32:26.

50. Cf. Bibliography.

51. Col. 29:8–10, trans. from Y. Yadin, 113.

52. R.E. Brown, *The Gospel According to John,* Vol. 1, p. 86.

53. Seven times if the blessings of breast and womb are counted as two.

54. *OTP,* Vol. 2, 819.

55. P. Minear, "The Beloved Disciple . . . "

56. Benjamin is given relatively little attention in Jacob's final blessing and testament in Genesis 49. Jacob merely states that "Benjamin is a ravenous wolf, in the morning devouring the prey, and at evening dividing the spoil" (49:26). This contrasts with the superabundant sevenfold blessing conferred on Joseph (49:22–26). Joseph also receives a double inheritance when Jacob adopts his two sons Ephraim and Mannaseh as his very own. In addition, he receives a special portion of land *more than his brothers* in Shechem (48:22). In the final blessing of Moses, Minear compares the beloved disciple in Jesus' bosom to Benjamin who "makes his dwelling between his shoulders" (Dt 33:12). However, the reference makes better sense describing God as making his dwelling (in a territorial sense) in the hills (shoulders) of Benjamin where the temple will later be built. This priestly and temple emphasis is very evident in the special blessing to Levi which precedes that of Benjamin.

57. Alan Culpepper treats of the similarity of the work of the Paraclete and the beloved disciple in his book, *Anatomy of the Fourth Gospel,* pp. 123–124.

58. Cf. Bibliography.

59. J.M. Ford has illustrated how a complete and sudden flow of blood was considered essential in the Jewish notion of sacrifice.

60. Pp. 320–321.

61. Girard's arguments are found in detail in his article in *Sciences Réligieuses.*

62. Brown, 1966, pp. 527–530.

63. This chapter is adapted from my article on Mary's role in the fourth gospel.

64. Giblin shows that this format is found in 2:1–11; 4:46–54; 11:1–44.

65. Brown, 1979, p. 169 describes one of the groups addressed by the gospel in this manner but does not connect it with this text.

66. The fact that Mary and the family exert their authority to call Jesus away in Mark 3:31 indicates that Joseph was already dead by the time that Mark's gospel was written, for such a matter would involve paternal authority.

67. P. 4.

68. *Anatomy of the Fourth Gospel,* pp. 123–124. This is taken from a theme developed in his previous book, *The Johannine School.* Cf. Bibliography.

69. In her unpublished study of John 12:1–8.

70. This central theme is brought out in the article by H. Weiss.

71. Brown, "Roles of Women . . . ," p. 693.

72. In his article on the influence of the Song of Songs on the New Testament.

73. From a newspaper article on his lecture in San Francisco, Sunday, February 9, 1986 in the *San Francisco Chronicle.*

74. Cf. Bibliography.

75. Schneiders, p. 92.

76. From his conclusion on p. 268.

77. Cf. Bibliography.

78. P. 94.

79. P. 97.

80. P. 16.

81. In his *Gospel According to John,* Vol. I, pp. l–li. The dependence of the fourth gospel on genuine historical tradition is also brought out by C.H. Dodd in his book on the *Historical Tradition of the Fourth Gospel.*

82. P. xix.

83. Pp. xx–xxi.

84. Cf. my article on the "Last Testament–Succession Background of Matt. 9:35–11:1."

85. P. 21.

86. Pp. 5–10.

87. Their identity is suggested by the same Greek words for "young

man," *neaniskos,* and "clothed," *peribleblēmenos,* in Mark 14:51 and 16:9. A study of this and other thematic similarities/contrasts is found in the article by H. Fledderman (cf. Bibliography).

88. In his article on the original functions of John 21.
89. Cf. note 84.
90. Brown, 1982, p. x.
91. *Ibid.,* pp. x-xi.
92. *Ibid.,* pp. x-xi.

Bibliography

Achtemeier, P.J., "An Elusive Unity: Paul, Acts and the Early Church," *Catholic Biblical Quarterly* 48 (1986) 1–26.

Barrett, C.K., "The Lamb of God," *New Testament Studies* 1 (1954), 210–218.

Bascom, R.A., *Prolegomena to the Study of the Itinerary Genre in the Old Testament and Beyond* (Ann Arbor: University Microfilms, 1986).

Braun, J.-M., "Saint Jean, la Sagesse et l'histoire," in *Neotestamentica et Patristica* (Leiden: E.J. Brill, 1962), 122–133.

Brown, R.E., *The Gospel According to John* (i-xii) (Garden City: Doubleday, 1966).

———, *The Gospel According to John* (xiii-xxi) (Garden City: Doubleday, 1970).

———, *The Community of the Beloved Disciple* (Ramsey: Paulist Press, 1979).

———, *The Epistles of John* (Garden City: Doubleday, 1982).

———, "Roles of Women in the Fourth Gospel," *Theological Studies* 36 (1975) 688–699.

Cambe, M., "L'Influence du Cantique des Cantiques sur le Nouveau Testament," *Revue Thomiste* 62 (1962) 5–26.

Charlesworth, J.H. (ed.), *Old Testament Pseudegrapha,* Vol. 1 (N.Y.: Doubleday, 1983).

Clark, D.K., "Signs in Wisdom and John," *Catholic Biblical Quarterly* 45 (1983) 201–209.

Coakley, J.F., "The Anointing at Bethany and the Priority of John," *Journal of Biblical Literature* 107 (1988) 241–256.

Culpepper, R.A., *Anatomy of the Fourth Gospel: A Study in Literary Design* (Philadelphia: Fortress, 1983).

———, *The Johannine School,* SBL Diss. Series 26 (Missoula: Scholars Press, 1975).

DeGoedt, M., "Un schème de révélation dans le quatrième évangile," *Novum Testamentum* 8 (1962) 142–150.

De La Potterie, I., "La tunique sans coutre, symbole du Christ grand prêtre," *Biblica* 60 (1979) 255–269.

Derrett, J.D.M., "Why Jesus Blessed the Children (Mk 10:13–16 PAR)," *Novum Testamentum* 25 (1983) 1–18.

Dodd, C. H., *Historical Tradition in the Fourth Gospel* (N.Y.: Cambridge University Press, 1963).

———, *The Interpretation of the Fourth Gospel* (N.Y.: Cambridge University Press, 1953).

Ellis, P., *The Genius of John* (Collegeville: Liturgical Press, 1984).

Ethedirge, J.D., *Targums of Onkelos and Jonathan Ben Uzziah with the Fragments of the Jerusalem Targum* (N.Y.: Ktav, 1968).

Filson, F.V., "Who Was the Beloved Disciple," *Journal of Biblical Literature* 68 (1949) 83–88.

Fitzmyer, J., *The Gospel According to Luke* (N.Y.: Doubleday, 1981).

Fledderman, H., "The Flight of a Naked Young Man (Mark 51–52)," *Catholic Biblical Quarterly* 41 (1979) 412–418.

Ford, J. M., " 'Mingled Blood' from the Side of Christ (John xix. 34)," *New Testament Studies* 15 (1968–69) 337–338.

Gerhard, J., *The Literary Unity and Compositional Methods of the Gospel of John,* unpublished dissertation (Washington: Catholic University of America, 1975).

Giblin, C., "Suggestion, Negative Response and Positive Action in St. John's Portrait of Jesus," *Catholic Biblical Quarterly* 26 (1980) 197–211.

Girard, M., "La composition structurelle des sept signes dans la quatrième évangile," *Sciences Réligieuses* 9 (1980) 315–324.

Glimm, Marique Walsh, *The Apostolic Fathers* (N.Y.: Heritage, 1947).

Grassi, J., "The Last Testament—Succession Literary Background of Matthew 9:35–11:1 and Its Significance," *Biblical Theology Bulletin* 7 (1977) 172–176.

Grassi, J., "The Role of Jesus' Mother in John's Gospel: A New Approach," *Catholic Biblical Quarterly* 48 (1986) 67–80.

Hoskyns, E., edited by Davey, N.D., *The Fourth Gospel* (London: Faber and Faber, 1947).

Käsemann, E., *The Testament of Jesus According to John 17,* trans. G. Krodel (Philadelphia: Fortress, 1968).

Kilgallen, J. "John the Baptist, the Sinful Woman and the Pharisee," *Journal of Biblical Literature* 104 (1986) 675–679.

Martyn, J.L., *History and Theology in the Fourth Gospel* (N.Y.: Harper, 1968).

Meeks, W., "The Image of the Androgynous Man: Some Uses of a Symbol in Earliest Christianity," *History of Religions,* 13 (1973) 165–208.

Minear, P., "The Beloved Disciple in the Gospel of John," *Novum Testamentum* 19 (1977) 105–123.

Minear, P., "The Original Functions of John 21," *Journal of Biblical Literature* 102 (1983) 85–98.

Munro, W., "Women Disciples in Mark," *Catholic Biblical Quarterly* 44 (1982) 225–241.

Neyrey, J., "The Jacob Allusions in John 1:51," *Catholic Biblical Quarterly* 44 (1982) 586–605.

Neyrey, J., "Jacob Traditions and the Interpretation of John 4:10–26," *Catholic Biblical Quarterly* 41 (1979) 419–437.

O'Grady, J.F., "The Role of the Beloved Disciple," *Biblical Theology Bulletin* 9 (1979) 58–65.

Pagels, E., *The Gnostic Gospels* (N.Y.: Vintage Books, 1981).

———, *The Johannine Gospel in Gnostic Exegesis: Heracleon's Commentary on John* (Nashville: Abington, 1973).

Parker, P., "John the Son of Zebedee and the Fourth Gospel," *Journal of Biblical Literature* 81 (1962) 35–43.

Perrin, N., *Rediscovering the Teaching of Jesus* (N.Y.: Harper & Row, 1967).

Robinson, J.M., ed., *The Nag Hammadi Library* (San Francisco: Harper & Row, 1981).

Rosenbaum, M., Silbermann, A.M. (trans.), *Pentateuch with Targum Onkelos, Haphteroth and Rashi's Commentary* (N.Y.: Hebrew Publ. Co., 1950).

Rowland, C., "John 1:51, Jewish Apocalyptic and Targumic Tradition," *New Testament Studies* 30 (1984) 498–507.

Sanders, J.N., "Those Whom Jesus Loved," *New Testament Studies* 1 (1954) 29–41.

Schneiders, S.M., "The Foot Washing (John 13:1–20). An Experiment in Hermeneutics," *Catholic Biblical Quarterly* 43 (1981) 76–92.

Schneiders, S.M., "The Face Veil: A Johannine Sign (John 20:1–10)," *Biblical Theology Bulletin* 13 (1983) 94–97.

Schwartz, J., "Jubilees, Bethel and the Temple of Jacob," *Hebrew Union College Annual* 56 (1985) 63–85.

Staley, J., "The Structure of John's Prologue: Its Implications for the

Gospel's Narrative Structures," *Catholic Biblical Quarterly* 48 (1986) 241–264.

Weiss, H., "Footwashing in the Johannine Community," *Novum Testamentum* 21 (1979) 298–325.

Winter, P., "Some Observations on the Language in the Birth and Infancy Stories of the Third Gospel," *New Testament Studies* 1 (1954) 111–158.

Woll, D.B., *Johannine Christianity in Conflict: Authority, Rank, and Succession in the First Farewell Discourse* (GA: Scholars Press, 1981).

Yadin, Y., *The Temple Scroll, the Hidden Scroll of the Dead Sea Sect* (N.Y.: Pandora, 1985).